The Reason Why I'm Living This Life

The Reason Why I'm Living This Life

MARIE MORRISON

Unless otherwise indicated, scripture quotations are taken from
the King James Version of the Bible – public domain.

Matador
9 Priory Business Park,
Wistow Road, Kibworth Beauchamp,
Leicestershire. LE8 0RX
Tel: 0116 279 2299
Email: books@troubador.co.uk
Web: www.troubador.co.uk/matador
Twitter: @matadorbooks

ISBN 978 1789018 905

British Library Cataloguing in Publication Data.
A catalogue record for this book is available from the British Library.

Printed and bound in the UK by T J International, Padstow, Cornwall
Typeset in 12pt Adobe Garamond Pro by Troubador Publishing Ltd, Leicester, UK

Matador is an imprint of Troubador Publishing Ltd

CONTENTS

Three

Four

Five

INTRODUCTION

THIS BOOK IS A COMPILATION OF personalised accounts expressing how and why many lives changed. There is a common misconception regarding those who attend church and have decided to dedicate their lives to God. Believe me when I say, we were not always like this. Some found themselves in predicaments they thought they could never escape, but it just goes to show that God can deliver anyone. I do not think people truly grasp where some of us are coming from and what God has saved us from. Some have been homeless, lost children, lost parents, drug abusers, drunkards, gang members, heavy smokers, self-harmers, gamblers – you name it, God saved them from it. Some had terminal illnesses and were told how little time they had left to live, but God intervened! A few of them were successful business people, and God stripped them right down to near enough nothing, so they could recognise who the true God was. Others came to the harsh reality that no amount of money could save their soul. Some just got tired of their lives spinning in circles; the drugs and alcohol seemed to help, but only for a time.

So yes, many were in a downward spiral. Irrespective of our race, gender or nationality, we can be saved; we all have a choice. One of the most powerful things God has given to humankind is free will. He will not force you to serve Him; He takes no pleasure in that and neither would you. We all knew something was missing, we just did not know that it was God.

It is funny – well, not funny ha-ha, but you know it is mind-blowing when people look at us believing that we were always this way, and you think, *If they ever knew!* Well, this book is written for you to know. God did not come to save the righteous because if He did, the church would be empty. We all have to begin somewhere, and this is how and where many stories began.

One

STANDING OUTSIDE THE PORTAL

HERE DO I BEGIN? WELL, I GOT saved in Gibson Road church; I do not even remember the time, but it was sometime in 1961 – yes, 1961. I just went to church to get my two babies blessed but, as usual when going to church, I believe, and it is a principle I stick to, that I should never go bare-headed. So, I had my hat on but I had my lipstick on too and my earrings in.

When I got to the church, I pushed the door and I peeped in. When I did so, I saw the choir in their surplices going up, and when I looked I didn't see any lipstick or earrings. I was not going to be the odd one out, so I closed the door, wiped the lipstick off my mouth, pulled the earrings out of my ears and went in. After I'd got the children blessed, I went to sit down and listened to the message. It was from Acts 2 and Bishop was preaching.

When the altar call was made I went, hands were laid on me and I prayed. It was like fire. *I am talking to you now and my body is getting goosebumps*, I said. I bawled at the altar; I bawled. I had a belly pain, it was terrible. My belly! I really, really cried out for my belly, it was so painful. Then the ministers of the church took me around the back. They talked to me about being baptised and I told them, 'Well, I can't get baptised because I am living with the babies' father and we're not married.'

So, they went and they called Bishop and he came and we talked, and he said, 'You must bring your husband-to-be in the night', and he came the Sunday night. We went back, went to Bishop's office and he spoke to us and asked if we loved each other and wanted to get married, and we said yes. They helped us to get married, so we got married on Saturday 10th October and were baptised on Sunday 11th October, which was my birthday.

Well, after a while the Enemy decided *You are not going to get away so easily*, so I had backslidden and for a long time I did not go to church. I used to see a lot of brethren and they really, really held me up, especially Sister Dorcas Campbell. She used to pinch and tump [thump] me: 'Yuh nuh see yuh nuh fit out deh [You don't see you do not fit out there]; why won't you come back to church?'

The one day I ran across Mother Whitton down Aston in her shop. Oh God! That was terrible. She said to me, 'Sister Evans, you can't come visit us, man? Even once a month you can't come up and visit us?' All that went on board, and I thought about it, thought about it, thought about it.

At the time, I was living at 138 Trinity Road in Aston, and anyway, I carried on partying and clubbing and all that went on until it just stopped. I was not going to any clubs, I was not going to any parties, I just went from work to home and one day I said to myself, *You know, I must go to church*. But before that, I was standing at the window upstairs and looking outside, and when I looked, it was as if I was the one outside, looking back at me inside. Then I heard these words: *Standing outside the portal, you are standing outside the door, knowing that with the demons forever you shall abide*, and I just came to myself and said, *I must go back to church, you know*.

So, it was coming up to Easter Sunday and I went to church. I went to church that Sunday and I am there until now, because when I went through the door that morning, the first person I saw was Sister Whitton, and when I got in afterwards I saw Mother Dunn. Oh, they welcomed me so much! I was dead scared of coming in here before, because I used to do the flowers in church and I had to go and get the key. I was so scared. So, Mother Dunn asked me one day, if I can cook sweet. But before she asked me, I was at home preparing dinner, and I was dishing out my son's meal. I cooked some cabbage and carrots for vegetables, and when I was putting it on the plate (you know I cook with a lot of butter when I am cooking vegetables), I heard a voice behind me – 'He doesn't take so much grease' – and a few weeks after that, Mother Dunn asked me to come and help one convocation. The sister that used to come and do it could not because she had to go away, so she asked a few more sisters and me to come, which we did.

That was 26th July 1962, and I am here until today. You know the first thing Mother Dunn told me when I was in the kitchen cooking was 'Bishop doesn't like a lot of grease, but he loves gravy' – and he does! As I saw that she needed help after convocation when everybody had gone, I promised that I would come and help her, and when I retired, I'd come full time and look after her and Bishop, and I am here until this blessed day. That is my story. I am saved; I am saved and saved again.

Eulalee Evans

I PROMISE I WILL GO BACK

I WILL TELL YOU HOW I WAS SAVED. I found that during the course of the day, I started to think about God, but I never read the Bible. I never really had a Bible – well, I had one somewhere. I remember I kept seeing *G-O-D* reoccur. I was in a relationship with someone at the time.

But I remember one night, I heard a voice say, *You're not going to win this fight*, and I turned around and there was nobody there. When I used to walk down the street I would think to myself, *I need to go to church, I know I need to go to a church*, and I remember saying to the Lord, *I do not want to go to a dead church*. So I walked and I looked and I was like *No, not that church… not that church*, and then I remember passing Gibson Road. I looked at them and I said, *I am not going to that church because them look too posh fi me* [they look too posh for me].

Then I remember when I was at college one woman was reading her Bible and she invited me to the Church of Prophecy, and I went. When she invited me she said she was going to pick me up, and I said, *I wish she did not come to pick me up now*, because I didn't want to go again. But because I promised her that I would go, I got ready and I went to church and I said, *Oh, this is all right*, and then I got baptised there. But I remember saying to myself, *I know I am going to get baptised again*, and I had a dream. After I had this dream, I went and bought myself a set of white clothes. I put them on top of my wardrobe and I said, *I know I am going to get baptised again*, and then I remember the Lord said to me, *You need to go to Israel*, and I asked if the church were going to Israel and they said they were going for six days. I said, 'No, I am not going to go for only six days.'

I used to work with Dawn Johnson and she said, 'Oh, we're going for eleven days', so I decided I would go with her. I used to pay her the money faithfully, but I never went to the church at the time. The day we left for Israel was the first time I met the brethren. I spent eleven days in Israel and the Word was so profound. Elder McLean was the one that was teaching.

When we came back, I started to go to the Bible class on Fridays. I remember one night, I heard a voice say to me, *You need to get baptised now*, and I replied, *But I am already baptised* and I left it at that. I went to Bible class on Friday and then when I got home a voice said to me, *You could have died this night!* and I was so frightened! I phoned Elder McLean and said, 'Elder McLean, I want to get baptised next Friday.' But it was the longest week ever because every day I thought I was going to die, until I was baptised.

Then after I was baptised, I was still going to the other church and I did not go to Gibson Road for about three months. Then I dreamt that there was a storm with doves, and I think somebody picked them up and crushed them. I said, *What does that mean?* I woke up and a voice said, *You took my name, but you're not wearing it!* I said to the Lord, *I promise I will go back; I will just go to this church one more time.*

So, I went to Prophecy one more time, and I never went back. I started to go to Gibson Road, and that is how I was saved.

Angelina Martin

TODAY

 WAS NOT UP YET, AND THE VOICE just spoke and I heard, *Today*.
I said, *Today what?*

The voice said, *Today*, so I just got busy and put my clothes on. I don't even know if I had anything to drink. I went right up to church and service was on. When the altar call came, I just got up and went to the altar. I was not baptised in the morning, but in the evening. You know, on Thursday nights, when service opened, there was prayer and a scripture reading. There was no preaching, and they said, 'Who is not filled with the Holy Ghost? Hands up', and I put my hands up, and as my knee touched the ground, I was filled. I started to work for the Lord the same time, and from that until now it is my job. Precious memories.

I am still in the fight; it is good, it is very, very, very good, it keeps me alive, keeps me going and believe you me, I will do it over and over again, because it's my life. The comforter is with me, yeah. In those days, it was a powerful, powerful time. You know, even before I was saved I used to visit just before they built the extension. I decided it was the last time I was going to visit and I never went back in there because it was too powerful. But the time had come when I heard the voice say, *Today*, and I'm still on the day of today, it will never leave me. So God helped me. I cannot play about, no, no, no, this is too precious, man, too precious. There were plenty, a whole lot of opportunities, but I let them go. I have Jesus. What want I more? He is everything to me.

When you get the call from God, it is good; when nobody forces you, or invites you, it is a call. Like a call come from Macedonia, but it was Heaven calling. It said, *Today*, and I am still listening to the voice saying, *Today*, so I try my best to live each day as today. Yes, it is a blessing and as I said before, I cannot play about. I could have really mixed up and played about, but I remember I got a call. The call is there. Today, today; not tomorrow, today! I do not mind who likes or dislikes me, I am just going on. But I tell you that it pays to serve Jesus. You may not have a lot in your pocket, or a whole lot to eat, but you have Jesus! We have so much to give God thanks for, so much, and I tell you this much: we have to try our best to do better than we are doing now, because we don't know what will happen tomorrow.

Charles Riley

GOD HAD A DIFFERENT PLAN

I GREW UP IN KINGSTON IN AUGUST Town, but I did not live a good life. My father died when I was seventeen, and at the age of eighteen, I became a member of the famous Jungle Twelve Gang. I believe that sometimes your surroundings can have an effect on your life. I was brought up well, half-day of school and half-day of trade, but when you follow bad company... I am telling you that your environment can make you or break you. There were two parties in Jamaica: the Jamaican Labour Party (JLP) and the People's National Party (PNP). I became an activist for the PNP, so I was fighting to gain power for the party. We used weapons such as guns, knives and machetes; basically anything that was dangerous. I was a gunman for twenty years before I came to England.

My plan was to come to England to become rich and famous. I came to rob some drugs men and get their money to go back home with riches. That was the plan I had with some friends in London, but little did I know that God had a different plan for me. I came to Birmingham and I started working, but I was still in gang life. I was invited to church plenty of times so I went and passed through, but there was no power. I just came out and smoked my spliff and drank my Guinness same way. But one day I met someone and I was invited to church in 2008. I spoke to her and she said she went to church, then she invited me and I said okay.

I came to Number 2, Gibson Road. I came here for one year and two months, and one day the Word got to me and I started crying. It was one day in September 2009 that the Word of God was spoken from the pulpit and it was as if the preacher was speaking directly to me. I felt it so much I began to cry; I was crying like a baby. I went to the altar crying and I told Elder Mac that I wanted to be baptised. I felt everything I ever did wrong come before me. Knowing how I was in my past life, I was carrying a load of sin and my burden was heavy. I needed rest for my soul! I said, 'I want to be baptised.' I was broken! I said, 'I don't want to go home unless I've been baptised. I love this church because they follow the protocol and they do it the right way. That is why I am here, you know. If Jesus was never here they could not hold me here; I am telling you the truth.' I was so tangled up and so wild! You couldn't tame me.

That day I was baptised and I felt light for two weeks! It was like a weight lifted off my shoulder. It was as if I was floating because the heavy burden was lifted, so I felt that this baptism was true. You know what? Before I was baptised, when I was asleep at night, the things I used to do, they used to come back and hold me and I used to jump up, I couldn't sleep! I ran from Jamaica but I couldn't run from myself. Night after night I had nightmares because of the evil I used to do, the wickedness, it came back to haunt me. We must be careful of the evil that we are involved in right now, I am telling you! Be careful because if you can lie down and sleep peacefully something is wrong, I can tell you that!

After one year and six months, I received the gift of the Holy Ghost, and from that time until now, I have no regret. I am going from strength to strength. When I sing '*I am redeemed*'[1] I do not sing it as a joke; I was bought with a price. I can now testify, sing and pray. I am just growing in God with the help of the saints and am grateful for the love that they show me. You see, if someone comes to this church and they don't receive love they will just turn back, but the love that I received, it felt like I had a family and I felt at home, so I continued to stay and grow and now there is nothing else for me but church. My strength comes from believing the Word by faith, obedience to the Word, and allowing the Word to be a lamp unto my feet and a light unto my pathway. Jesus told the disciples that believed in Him, *If ye continue in my Word, then are ye my disciples indeed; And ye shall know the truth, and the truth shall make you free* (St John 8:31–32, King James Version).

In closing, I want to assure the reader that baptism in Jesus' name does work, and that is why I am here today! Now I am free from sin and have Christ within.

God bless.

Two

WHAT HAVE YOU GOT TO LOSE?

I HAD HEARD OF GOD BUT DID NOT really *know* Him. Many times I had heard Mum, Sister Ivy Brown, praying in the night-time, daytime, any time! But I never really knew God for myself.

I lived in Italy for many years, working as an airport controller and as a translator for some of the big tour operators. I travelled all over the world; in fact, over eleven years I went to thirteen or fourteen countries but settled in Amalfi on the southern Italian coast, where I was going to make a life for myself. I had, I believed, a good job, nice apartment, company car, laptop, phone, etc., etc. Life, I thought, was good; I was planning to get married and bring my mum over to Italy as the weather was amazing and the fresh food would do her good. It was my way of saying, 'Thank you, Mum.' This was my plan for my life. My dad had passed away eight months prior, and by the following month, my mother had also passed away. Within three years, on the day after what would have been my father's birthday, my son would be murdered. I knew he was in danger but could not do anything. God showed me He was going to take my son. It was to prepare me; that was in May 2010, and by June 2010, my son had been murdered, but God kept me. I did not realise at the time, but it had to have been God.

It was an ordinary long day at Naples Airport. I had been there all day. I had to send my flight reports back to the UK duty office (a task I did not like doing, as it took ages). I poured myself a glass of Chianti and sat at the laptop doing flight reports, then I heard a small voice, and it was so, so comforting.

Voice: *Why do you drink?*

Me: *Because I can.*

Voice: *But you do not even like it.*

Looking at the glass of red wine, I said, *Yeah, I know*; then I heard, *So stop!*

From that point, I just stopped drinking alcohol. At the same time I realised what I had just said, and the fact that I had had a conversation with someone who was only a voice. I was perplexed, but not afraid. I could not quite understand, and I thought, *Maybe I am just tired*, but something inside me knew there was more to this.

So, in the space of a few months, I lost it all. Everything happened so fast. I say it was a few months but even now, looking back five years, the time span still does not make sense. It seemed physically impossible to have all that happen in that short amount of time, *but it did*.

I was back in the UK, homeless, unemployed and I did not know how long my money was going to last. I found a bed and breakfast in Crawley, Sussex, and stayed there a couple of weeks whilst trying to find work as my money was running out. Finally, my money did run out, but the landlady was so kind she let me stay an extra night and I left in the morning. I was so depressed, I did not know what to do or where to go. I stood with my two suitcases, my backpack and my laptop case. I could not think any more; everything sounded like noise. I could not cry. I felt so lost and alone. Was this how I was going to end up? Destitute, alone on the street?

But just as I was about to give up, I saw a hand, a right hand, open right in front of me and heard a soft voice coming from it saying, *Come*.

From then, things just miraculously turned around. My cousin in Birmingham called and said, 'Come to Birmingham. I am sending a paid ticket, just get to the coach station.' Even in my desperate situation, hungry and lost, alone and homeless, I still did not want to go to Birmingham. I used to say that the best thing about Birmingham was the road, and here I was having to go there! I can only laugh about it now, but at the time, it was punishment. I travelled around Birmingham with my cousin Barbara and stayed at her house for a few months. Then I got a room in a house in Selly Oak. The woman who took the rent was an awful bully, but the room was big and I could lock my door. While travelling around with my cousin, we were in a place called Handsworth, Soho Road, and she casually said, 'Bishop Dunn has a big church down there', and I thought, *It cannot be the same Bishop Dunn who I had met years ago as a child.*

One day in June 2012, I went to bed. It was an ordinary day. I went to sleep, then got up, and the first thing I thought was *I want to go to church.* I remembered my cousin saying, 'Bishop Dunn has a big church down there.' But then I thought, *Down there where? I do not know Birmingham; how would I find the church?* Then I heard that still, small voice again: *Bev, you travelled the world by yourself sometimes; when you get off the plane all you have is a pack and it directs you to your hotel. You mean to say you cannot find a church in the same city you're in?* So I got up and Googled Bishop Dunn, and sure enough there was a telephone number. I thought, *I can't just ring*, and then I thought, *Yes I can*, so I did and a lady answered. I now know it was Mother Evans. She said hello, and I just said I wanted to come to church. She told me to get the Number 16 to Gibson Road.

So Sunday morning, I got up and then I realised I had no church clothes. I had fabulous clothes when

I was living in Italy, lovely designer stuff; shoes, handbags, but no church clothes, and I was not going to wear trousers. It was a disaster. *So*, I thought, *let me do the best I can.* So I did my make-up, put on my wig and earrings; the nails were still looking good, and I walked out the door and off to church.

I got to Birmingham town centre fine. I got on the Number 16, but the bus driver said he did not know where Gibson Road was. I said, 'What?! You're a bus driver and you don't know your roads?' He looked at me as if I was crazy. No, let me explain. I came from a small village called Minor Amalfi, where the Sita bus drivers know the roads and everybody, and where everyone lives. Every time I see the Galaxy chocolate advert it reminds me of the harbour in Amalfi. So I was shocked that this driver didn't know. I sat down at the back of the bus, disheartened, and I thought, *Oh well, I will just go for a ride, then go home.* What I had noticed was that there were other 'church people' (as I called them) on the bus, but they were getting off at the Baptist church. I could have got off with them, but I believe God did not allow it to register even though they were right in front of me, getting off the bus to go to church.

As they got off, some other church people got on the bus. Just as the bus started to move, I heard that still, small voice again: *Sit on the right side of the bus.* I thought, *Do I do it, or do I just sit here?* I heard it again

– Sit on the right-hand side of the bus – so I hesitated and then got up and sat on the other side. Just as I did, I saw the sign for Gibson Road and the other people were getting up as well, so I was so happy. I got off the bus and was crossing the road when a thought came to me, so tangible I could have almost touched it: *You can't go to church; where do you think you're going? They are church people, they belong in church but not you – you smoke, you drink, you had a boyfriend; you can't go in there.* I became afraid and felt so ashamed that I really thought that I could not go in God's house, I just couldn't. So I started to take really tiny steps to let the church people go on ahead so I could just turn around and cry and go back home, but as I was doing so, a man, Brother Bailey, turned around and, in his happy, chirpy voice, said, 'You coming church?'

I felt a sudden rush of joy and said, 'Yes! I'm coming to church' and hastened my footsteps, but as I got to the gates my legs became so heavy; it was like walking through quicksand. The church people had gone ahead. My legs wouldn't move and I started to panic; my heart was beating really fast, but I was still trying my best to move my legs. Nothing was happening. I remember just looking at the church doors and focusing on them. I had to get to the doors! I had to get inside the church; my life depended on getting inside. I remember saying to myself, *Bev, if you don't get into the church, you're going to die.* I remember saying, *I don't care if it is full in there,*

I will sit on the floor, I don't care, but I have to get inside.

The heavy feeling just lifted. As I walked inside I felt a presence; I can't put it into words, but I am going to try. It felt like the breath of warmth as you open the front door on a freezing cold day, that warm feeling as if to say, *Welcome home, my child.* In all my years, I had never, ever felt that before in my life like I did as I walked into Bethel United Church of Jesus Christ Apostolic, 2 Gibson Road, Birmingham, England. I knew then that I was home. This was what God wanted and where He wanted me to be, to bring me home.

I remember Elder Fisher preaching and I was feeling really uncomfortable. Then at the end of his sermon, he said for everyone to stand. I was sitting with Sister Hyacinth Bailey, Brother Bailey's wife; they had kind of taken me under their wing and I felt like an adopted daughter – they were so kind to me, and still are. So I also stood up and I was pacing from one foot to the other but I didn't realise I was doing it. Then I thought, *Why do I feel so uncomfortable?* It was like something was stirring inside me. I thought, *I've got to get out of here, I need to go,* but Elder Fisher hadn't finished talking and there was only the altar call and closing prayer left. It would be rude to walk out before the end of service and my mother wouldn't have been pleased, so I said to myself, *Hold on, Bev, it's not long.* I'm still pacing from one foot to the other and this feeling inside of me is getting stronger. Elder Fisher was ministering a prophetic word to a woman right across the other side of the auditorium, and anyone who knows Bethel Convention Centre knows how big it is. Then this woman started to cry and scream, and I was thinking, *How can she act like that in public? It's not the done thing for a woman.*

But as I was thinking this (and this was one of those life-changing moments), I heard what I can only describe as the sound of a mighty, rushing wind coming in my direction. I heard it coming, it was fast and powerful, and it got me so quick I didn't even realise. All I remember is I had my hands in the air screaming, 'Oh God, oh God, oh God', and I couldn't stop.

I could hear Sister Bailey: 'He is breaking her down, God is breaking her down', and that was exactly what was happening.

Three months later, I was baptised on the 23rd September 2012, the same day my mother had passed away about five years before. It was a choir song that broke me, and when Elder Jones said six words to me: 'What have you got to lose?' On the day of my baptism there was a prophecy; I will never forget it. *I am with thee always, even unto the end of the world.* God changed my life around. If He can do it for me, He can do it for you too.

Beverley D'luci

PHASE 1: CONCLUDING CHOICE

Okay, so let me weigh the options, and see if I was to
    take this road.
What would I have to give up? My friends, my money,
    my gold?
I contemplate and think deeper – my life! What do I
    want for it?
This world still has a lot to offer, and with it my soul
    has long been knit.

To cut this cord I've been attached to will cause such
    discomfort and pain,
The blood, sweat and tears from parting will leave such
    a distasteful stain.
Yet, if I stay connected, taking my last breath, what will
    my final state be?
I will know I should have destroyed the cord, long
    before it had done so to me.

The soul ties keep me entangled, I cannot seem to make
the break,
But am I persuaded to cut this bond, as it is my soul
that is at stake?
Cutting the tie is one thing; it's also the fear of entering
a realm that is new,
Then I recall so many warnings, knowing my time to
surrender is well overdue.

In my current state, peace and sleep are abandoned; it
is the common theft.
I often find myself asking, *What if the trump has
sounded? What if I have been left?*
My fears of being deserted could relinquish, if I but
only make this right choice,
Oh, the joy and tranquillity I know I'm missing; why
can't I just take heed to His voice?

I see that there are two ways set before me, so do I stay
or do I cut loose?
Desiring to leave this world, knowing my purpose of
being was put to its rightful use.
I just don't know whether I will see tomorrow; it's like
I'm gambling, rolling a dice,
Now I've made my choice and decided, for to lose my
soul is too steep a price.

USEFUL INSTEAD OF USELESS

GREW UP IN KINGSTON. I HAD NO family; no mother and no father. I ran away when I was very small because my mother died and my father wasn't a man that cared. He married again and they both didn't care, so that is when everybody went their own ways. So I decided to go and live in Kingston. I worked with many, many people, very good people. I took to smoking, and that was my life. I did not know any other. Everybody was frightened of me; I had a loud mouth and I could frighten anybody. I used to pick up the back of a car to get a shilling, and I used to lift up a bag of rice with my teeth just to show off, as I was very, very strong. People used me to do anything as they wanted to make money off me. So, that was me in the world. You see, I never grew up with a family; what I had is what I got from people. My dad used to live with a woman and they just used to fight, but I liked it when they did because every time they had a fight and she cooked, she cooked loads, and they didn't eat it so we went and ate it all.

I decided I didn't want that life, but I asked the Lord for the life I have now. In 1951 everything was happening. I remember there was a storm, and it was the same year I met my wife, who was my girlfriend at the time. I wanted something, but I didn't know what it was. I could not have a meal unless I smoked a cigarette. My cigarettes were in my breast pocket all the time. So if my wife went to the shop to buy anything, she knew she had to get a pack of cigarettes for me because I could not eat the food unless I had a cigarette. I was bad; I mean, I was bad, I tell you. I never used to have one girl, but I had many. Every Saturday night I met somebody else and I went on with that lifestyle until I became sick of it. I used to steal, but the way I did it, nobody would notice. I remember I was a liar; I was a good liar. My life was miserable. I done everything that I felt I could do. I went to the dance and the dance finished; I went to the pictures and come back. I just done things to keep me active.

I had been baptised before in the name of the Father, Son and Holy Ghost, but at the time, I did not take any thought of what name or title I was baptised in. One day I heard a noise from a church and they were shouting, 'Hallelujah!', and I said, *This must be the*

Devil in here because it was so loud and they were just going on.

I went by the door and looked through the window. As I went to the window and looked in, this lady came up, a missionary. She said, 'Hello, sir', and I said, 'Hello', and she said, 'Do you want to go to the altar?' I really wanted to go, but I was hesitant. I did not know how people came to the church and went to the altar; I was afraid of Christian people and the pulpit, I was afraid of them. But I went in, and she said, 'Give me your bicycle.' She took my bicycle from me and put it around the corner, and I went to the altar.

You know, you think about others being in church, but not yourself. For me, I never expected to be in church. Church was not my style. I went back to the church and the man asked me if I wanted to be baptised, and I said, 'I am already baptised.'

He said, 'What are you baptised in?'

I said, 'I don't know, but I am baptised.'

He said, 'Where is the church?' and I told him, and he said, 'That's Father, Son and Holy Ghost, people', and the minute he told me that, something in me was touched, so I told him I would come back and get baptised on Sunday, and that was the Wednesday.

So, when I came home I went and I smoked Friday, Saturday and Sunday. When I went for the baptism, I still had five cigarettes in my pocket, because I did not think I could give up the habit that easily. When I was baptised, they said they were going to have tarrying on Monday at seven o'clock. So when I went to work I didn't have any peace, no peace at all. I did not want any food. I went to church at seven o'clock and by 7.15, I was speaking in tongues. God touched me and done something to me. I met a sister and she said to me, 'Brother, God touched you tonight, but you need the power, all you want is the power', because I spoke in tongues and I could not stop. When I got home, I realised that I really needed the power.

On my way home, I went to the shop to buy a sweetie. (That was after I got the Holy Ghost.) I put the sweetie in my mouth as a substitute, and immediately, it was the first time the Lord spoke to me. I never knew that God could speak to somebody. He said to me, *You did not stop yourself from smoking cigarettes; I stopped you from smoking cigarettes!* I was frightened, and I opened my mouth – there were tears and the sweet dropped from my mouth, and from then on nobody could smoke in my house.

When I was living downtown, I went to every club. I was a part of a gang of young people, and I thought, *How can I go and tell them now that I am saved; how am I going to deal with that?* When I went home that night, I was sitting down because I didn't have anywhere to sleep. I said, *Well, I can't go back and sleep with the lady I was courting.* So I took up my Bible and I put it in front of my eyes because I was ashamed to let them know that I had gone to church.

When I lifted up my arms and put my Bible before me, I said, *Lord, what is going to happen to my life now?* Then suddenly I saw a light. It was the brightest light that I had ever seen; it came down from Heaven, it sat on my head and I spoke in tongues all night. I then got bold enough to speak to anybody. I spoke to all of them and they were converted, and every time they had seen me they said, 'It is you that caused me to be here.'

Nobody expected that I would be saved. When I went to church, God just filled it with people because a lot of people followed me. I then realised that I was keeping back a crowd of people from going to church.

My soon-to-be wife came to church the same month, and she was baptised but didn't receive the Holy Ghost. I believe you have to pray to God to get what you want, so I just got up one Sunday and said, *I want to get married*, but I knew that I would never get married to a woman without the Holy Ghost. Everybody was asking, 'Brother Martin, did she receive the Holy Ghost?' and I said, 'No.' That night we went to a church in a place they call Stoney Hill and God knocked her out in the Spirit. When I saw the Holy Ghost work I said, 'That's the lady', and then everybody looked at me and said, 'That's the Holy Ghost.' That is what I wanted. I wanted to get married, but she had to get the Holy Ghost first and then I married her, and we've been together now for sixty-five years.

On the Sunday morning, we got married and I bought her ring, along with other things she wanted because she didn't have anybody and I didn't have anybody. She came from Port Antonio, then we met and we just became one. I told them I was going to get married on the 10th September because my daughter was born on that date and I wanted to get married on her birthday. But I waited, and once August had arrived I said, 'I want to get my wife and I want to get married now, please', so I didn't get married on the 10th September, I got married on the 10th August.

My pastor said, 'You are privileged.'

Life for me was not comfortable. There were so many things that I had to get rid of. I used to gamble and I used to play bingo; I just loved bingo and I loved playing cards. Eventually, I got rid of the money I got whilst I was gambling. I was done, I was sick of using it. I had a good business in Jamaica and I used to make plenty of money. I banked with Barclays, I owned two cars and one van, and I gave my wife two maids, one to cook and one to wash; but I decided to come to England.

When I came to England, I was on £10 a week – £10 a week! I cried, I told my wife and said, 'Let me come home', and she said, 'No, no – let me come to you.' She came three months later, and four months after that she sent for the children, so all of us were here within seven months.

I went to her sisters in Small Heath and I wanted to find a church. I said, *Jesus, where is the church?* He said, *Go to the marketplace.* So I went and asked my sister-in-law, 'Where's the marketplace?'

She said, 'The Bull Ring; the Number 16 bus will take you there', so I went to the Bull Ring.

I went to the market, I leaned over and someone said, 'Brother Martin!' and it was a man from the Church of God. He took me home to his house and I preached Jesus' name. I was there all day Saturday and I was hungry. About six o'clock they came down for dinner and I had seen a piece of shin in the pot cooking, and the colour of the pumpkin in the soup looked good. They blessed the dinner and I sat down.

I took one spoonful and said, 'I'm sorry, I can't drink it', and I moved from the table.

They said, 'Why do you say you can't drink it? It's good!'

I said, 'Unless you repent and are baptised in Jesus' name, you're going to Hell. What I want is to baptise you in Jesus' name now and for you to baptise your church members because nobody can go to Heaven without it.'

The man said, 'You know who you're looking for? The Jesus only church.' I said, 'Where?'

And he said, 'I'm not going to tell you, unless you have the soup.'

He gave me the spoon and I began to drink the soup, and I said, 'Thank you very much. Well, all right now, I'm drinking the soup.'

Then he told me about Gibson Road church.

Let nobody fool you, darling: when you come to this church, you come to God Himself; you don't come to Elder Martin, or Bishop Dunn, or Bishop So-and-So. All you want is for us to lead you to Jesus; if we're not showing you that, it's not for your company. The God you talk to is not dumb, He is alive, and all you have to do is go on your knees and say, *Jesus, I want to hear something about you; tell me anything.* If you live in a house with me and my wife and we're not talking, that's not fellowship. You need to have God in you to tell you, *This is right, my child.* Don't be satisfied until He tells you something. He must tell you where to go, when to move and when to do the things that you should do. Salvation is your own with you and God alone. No matter how close a person is to you, it is you and Him. My wife and I live together, and if the Rapture comes, I tell her all the time that we become one flesh but not one spirit, so if something is not right and you follow me and do it, you're going to Hell.

The more you know about Jesus, the more nobody can fool you. You see, when you know you love the Lord and He begins to talk to you, you differ from everybody. You will have trouble, because nobody will want to hear you, but that's good because you have to fight and be brave in the face of all evil; you never run and never lag behind, so you need to make it. Paul talked about saints – we *are* saints. People come to church and say they're Christian but they don't have the lifestyle. Saints are different from Christians; everybody I bump into says they are a Christian. They say, 'I go to church too', but they don't have anything to show for it. When you become a saint, you have got something to show. Everybody must know that you've been changed. I believe that people that are converted must change, but we cannot change alone.

I've got to go to Heaven. I don't want anybody to miss this, because it will be a great time. We've got to see Jesus. But you've got to have somebody to help you. Don't watch what everybody does; it is your spirit that works with God. He has given you the Spirit, and if you go to do anything that is contrary the Spirit will wake you up and say, *Why are you doing it?* and that's God's Spirit. If you give up your little life to Him, He will work it out for you. So my life was not like any of yours. I was like a wild dog. God picked me up from out of a dump and I'm proud every time I see my family – nine children, eighteen grandchildren and eleven great-grandchildren. My life was changed by God Himself because He took me and changed my whole life. He made me useful instead of useless.

Gladstone Martin

THE FINAL PIECE OF MY JIGSAW

ELL, IT HAS BEEN A BIT OF A FIGHT to get to the point in my life where I feel that I can share my testimony openly. That opportunity has now arisen. I no longer share my testimony with pain and fear, but I tell my story with boldness, thanksgiving and pride that I have come through and God has never ceased to amaze me.

I was not a churchgoer and I did not come from a religious background; the extent of my knowledge of God was the biblical films my mom would watch every Easter and Christmas, harvest festivals at school, and my nan who went to church and for a short time took me to Sunday school a couple of times. Beyond that I had no care for God or religion. My childhood was a dark time in my life. I grew up without knowing my biological father. However, my stepfather has been the only constant in my life, and he is the only father I know. My stepfather, a drunk who was very abusive physically, emotionally and mentally to my mother, my sister and myself, was a troubled man who in truth hated black people. So much so that he would very rarely call me by my name; it would be 'Baboon Meat' or 'Nigger' for most of my childhood. I witnessed my mother being beaten up, raped in her sleep, and being constantly degraded.

I was blamed every time my mother was beaten, and told that it was my fault she was bleeding or bruised, and that if I were not around then it would all stop. I was beaten and mentally abused; fear was the main constant in my life. A fear of being killed in my sleep, of my sister or my mother being hurt. I was threatened daily with the possibility of being assaulted in some way, shape or form, or if not me, then my mom. I was afraid to sleep, as he would watch me from my doorway and threaten to suffocate, rape, stab or cut me, or just stand and laugh in my doorway.

I was constantly scared and torn; I felt so desperately guilty for being alive because I felt I caused my mom so much pain. I felt rejected and fearful most of the time, to the point that at a very young age I began to drink alcohol, smoke weed and self-harm. I tried everything and anything to take the feeling away.

When I was in my teens, I went to college and met a friend who told me she went to church, and would constantly invite me to come along. My response was always that I didn't believe in God. God was not real, or if He was, He was an evil God for letting bad things happen to people and never helping them. I was so angry whenever God was mentioned, because in my eyes He was a failure.

It was during my first year of college that I finally gave in because my friend was so persistent. I agreed that I would go to church just once, but she had to agree to stop asking me after that because I'd had enough of her pestering me all the time.

I walked through the church doors one Sunday afternoon, and an overwhelming feeling came over me. I could not explain it, but the feeling was so powerful that it broke me. I broke down in tears. I could not for the life of me understand what was going on, and I was so angry with myself for getting so upset after all of my resistance to going.

During that service every song that was sung spoke to me; every word spoken was like it was just directed at me, as if I were the only one in the building. I was totally dumbfounded. My friend asked if I would like to go again for the next service, and I said that I would. The following week I went and the exact same thing happened to me: an altar call was made and the invitation to give my life to Christ. I was fighting so hard not to move as I felt an unbelievable pull. However, I remained in my seat, sobbing, knowing what I had to do, but too scared to move.

I told my friend that I would go back the following week, and again the same thing happened to me. I was completely broken; I went to the altar and at that point the invitation was given to me and I said yes to Jesus. I was at the altar and I literally saw myself: my body was made up like a jigsaw, and the very centre of me was an empty black hole. When I said the name of Jesus, the final piece of my jigsaw was filled. God completely restored me at that moment.

This is a snippet of the beginning of my journey. Much had happened to me before my walk and much has happened during my walk with Him. I have learnt that God never fails, never gives up and never leaves me. God is a restorer, a deliverer and a miracle-working God.

I have seen first hand what the power of God can do. He turned my stepfather around from hating black people to now being an advocate and a voice for them. God has touched his heart and turned him around. God has softened my heart so that I can say I love the father I once hated, and have been freed from the turmoil of my past. My story has not ended, it's not over, but I know that through Christ all things are possible.

God bless.

YOU'VE GOT TO BELIEVE

WHEN I WAS LIVING IN JAMAICA, where I was sent to church depended on who I lived with. If I was living with my grandma I would go to the Catholic church, but when I was in town with my mom she would send us to the church across the road. We were living in Jones Town and sometimes we would go to other churches too. My siblings and I were about eight, six and four, and the three of us would go to church on Sundays. I think I went to church with my mom once. It was a church in Kingston and we were all dressed to the nines because we had all these lovely American dresses. I met my dad when I was nine and I went to live with him for a short while; he was a Seventh-Day Adventist. Somebody took me to see the crucifixion when I was about eight and when I saw it I was heartbroken; I couldn't understand why Jesus died. I felt sorry for Him.

A few years passed and I came to England when I was thirteen. I was with a group of children all coming over to meet our parents. We came on the plane by ourselves and the crew looked after us. When we arrived, we lived on Douglas Road off Grove Lane and the landlady was very nice. When she was going out she always said to me, 'I'm going to the bookies', so I said to her, 'Well can you put a bet on for me as well?' and she said yes. So I gave her a pound and she put a bet on a horse and I let her bet on some horses for me a couple of times but she didn't win any money, so I thought, *What a waste of time* and didn't bet on horses any more.

At the age of fourteen, I went to Handsworth Wood Girls' School. The English class that I was in had thirteen white girls and three black girls. One of the white girls said, 'Do you want to come to church with me one Sunday?' and I said yes. So I went to church with her and when I got there I was the only black person in the whole church, and as a fourteen-year-old and the only black person I felt uncomfortable and unwelcome. So I said to myself that I wouldn't go back, I felt embarrassed. I said to my mom, 'I am not going to go to any more churches because it's always the same: you go in the same and you come out the same way.' I didn't see the point in going. I stayed home and said, 'That's it – no more church for me.'

When I was fifteen, I thought, *Well, I'm fifteen now; I am going to get some make-up*, so I went up to Woolworths on Soho Road. Soho Road was different then from what it is now; there were lots of clubs and cinemas along the road, and it was Handsworth's high street at the time. So I bought lipstick, eyeshadow and nail varnish and I put them on my dressing table, because where we were living, I was living downstairs in the front room and my parents lived upstairs in another room. I was so embarrassed, I didn't want anyone to look at me so I didn't ever put them on, it was just there. I never did get to wear them. Every time I knelt down to pray, I'd put them in the drawer. Then one day I went to kneel down to pray, and I just got up and threw the make-up in the bin.

One day, my aunt came to the house and she said to me that she was going to this church and would I like to go with her? I said yeah, because I was used to going out with her back in Jamaica so I thought it would be all right. I went to church that Sunday night, I think it was June 1966, and I didn't know anything about the Apostolic church. I just sat down and listened and then an evangelist was calling people. My auntie said, 'Don't you see them calling people to the altar; why don't you go?'

So I went up there and the evangelist said to me, 'Do you want to be baptised?' Bearing in mind I was only fifteen, but they thought I was older as I looked it.

I wasn't sure about getting baptised as my mom was not there, but I decided to get baptised that night. Then I was thinking, *This is only water, it can't do anything.* So, I went home and told my mom I got baptised, and she went mad!

I used to meet three girls on Soho Road and walk to school with them. I said to them, 'Do you know, I went to church last night? I went to Bishop Dunn's church and I got baptised, but you don't have to worry because I'll be just the same. I'm not going to change or anything, it's only water; it can't do anything. I'll be all right.' We used to read *Ebony* magazine, and I said, 'I'll still be reading my *Ebony* magazine, I'll be all right.' So we went to school; we used to go early and play.

One day I went to school and one girl said to me, a couple of weeks after I got baptised, 'We don't want you to play with us any more because you're a Christian now.' So I just turned around and walked away because it didn't bother me, because I was happy with Jesus. I used to go to school and sit down and read my Bible in the corner by myself. They didn't really speak to me any more after that; they only said, 'Morning' and 'Evening' and had nothing else to do with me.

As a shortcut, I used to walk home from school through the park, and one day, one of the girls met me there to fight me. I decided I was not going to retaliate, because I am not really a fighter to be honest and I'd never been in a fight before. I just didn't like fighting as I felt you should be kind to people. So, while she attempted to fight me I didn't respond and she said, 'Oooh, that's the way a Christian should be', and then she walked away.

Another day I walked through the park and I had gone through the gate on Holly Road. I met another girl out there. She grabbed me by my hair, because my hair was longer at that time, and she was pulling me around by my hair saying, 'Why have you gone to church and gotten baptised?' She ran off and didn't speak to me again.

The girls in school continued to give me a hard time, saying, 'She won't be going to church for long.' So I had challenges at school after I was baptised.

When I started going to church I didn't get to go to Sunday school straight away as I had to do the Sunday dinner before I went to church and I didn't finish on time. I then started to get up earlier to cook the Sunday dinner so I could go to church early. I remember the first Golden Text that I heard when I went to church was *Let him that stole, steal no more: but rather let him labour, working with his hands the thing which is good, that he may have to give to him that needeth* (Ephesians 4:28, King James Version).

One Sunday morning Bishop was leading the service, as he used to moderate all the time, and he raised this song, Let Jesus Fix it for You. I was there, singing away, and then I was knocked out and I don't know what happened to me. When I recovered I was on the floor and I didn't know what the experience meant. When they said that I should tarry for the Holy Ghost I just kept going and I had different experiences. I remember one time I went to the altar and I was tarrying, and I could feel a pain in my belly and I felt as if I was way out in the country; it was like a meadow. It was lovely. When I looked at the top of the hill I could see an empty cross on the hillside. But you know I didn't understand, so I just kept going to the altar and tarrying.

Then one day I decided to become a nurse. I said, *Well, I don't fit in at church, so I'm going to become a nurse and I'm not coming back to church*, but I didn't tell that to anybody; it was just in my heart. The thing is, all the other young people were in the Spirit all the time and I wasn't. Mind you, I had a lot of joy. Even though I had joy they said, 'You have to do this and do that to be filled with the Holy Ghost', and I didn't match up to what they were saying and I just felt inferior. So anyway, before I left Bishop told the chorus group to collect some money for me and they bought me a watch. It was the first watch I ever had, and they gave me some money that helped to buy my lunch at the nursing home as student nurses lived there. I used to have a little job in Woolworths because that's where the teenagers usually went to work and they gave you a fiver for a whole week, working from Monday to

Friday, nine to six, so I saved a bit of that and that's what I went into nursing with.

One morning I woke up in the nursing home and everywhere I turned I saw Jesus hanging on the cross and I realised I had to go back to church. One day we were sitting in church and Bishop wanted some work done and said the brethren should come down and help. All the brothers were sitting on the right side and the sisters on the left side; they never mixed. I was sitting on the sisters' side on the front bench with a few other young people – I think I was about eighteen at the time. This evangelist came over and said, 'Some of you come and pray in this room and tarry', so we just followed her, we didn't argue. She told us that we should fast four days a week and we did... well, some of us did. Even when we were at school we fasted, and some people went into the toilets to pray. Though I wasn't in the mood, I knelt down to pray in obedience but I couldn't think of anything to say. I just said, *Jesus, Jesus*; I don't think I said it six times before I heard myself speaking in tongues. I was speaking and speaking and speaking and it felt as if I was in a different country. I could see the trees moving and I could feel the gentle breeze as well, it was so cool. The more I spoke in tongues, the more I felt myself going deeper into another realm.

I used to go home at lunchtime and kneel down in my room and pray. I found that every time I did so, my mom kept standing over me, wanting me to go to the shop, to do this and do that. So I said to myself, *I am not going to come home again in my lunch hour*. I decided I had to go and find somewhere to pray. So, I went down to the church in my school uniform, knocked on Bishop's door, and he came out and said, 'Sister, dear, what can I do for you?'

I said, 'Bishop, can I borrow the church key? I need to go and pray in the church', and to my surprise he gave it to me. And that's what I did every time; every lunchtime I just went down to church and prayed on my own. I was so heartbroken at the altar when I thought about Jesus and His suffering, I just cried, you know, I just cried and cried.

I joined the chorus group when I was sixteen. I remember one Sunday morning I was in church, and I left the choir and I knelt down to pray. I had a zeal for church. I was sitting down and the superintendent came over to me and said, 'I want you to become the assistant secretary for the Sunday school department.' So, I started writing the minutes from then, from the '60s. Then I had a lot of breaks because I got married and had the children and all that, but Sister Cynthia called me back.

At times when I got anointed and went down to the altar I still didn't think that I was filled, even when, as soon as I knelt down, I would start speaking in tongues and would get up and start dancing all over the place, but I still didn't think I was filled. One day when I looked back over my life I said, *Oh, but I'm filled*. It just dawned on me, but it took me years to realise that I *was* filled, and at that moment I started to believe. If you've got the Holy Ghost and you don't believe it doesn't work; you've got to believe! I didn't believe all those years that I was filled, and I couldn't understand why. It was because I was comparing myself to other people and listening to what other people were saying. From then on, I started to feel the Spirit, but it took me a long time.

Yeah, so this is it – God is my keeper, God is my saviour and my redeemer in Jesus' name. God changed my life very quickly, you know; I am surprised how quickly he changed my life and gave me joy. The joy of the Lord – that is what kept me, really.

God bless.

Three

A NEW HEART

I T WAS ALMOST NEW YEAR AND MY wife Ruby was at watch night. I went to her church but I was not a member; I was a visitor. But that December I went out on a spree and something happened to me. I went home and I asked my wife to get my breakfast as I was going to church Sunday, but somehow Ruby never responded. I was not going to Gibson Road church; I was going out to that Baptist church on Hamstead Road. On Sunday morning, I got up, put my clothes on and went, but it was too cold in the church so there was no service. My intention was to have my breakfast and stop in the public house because I did not want to drink on an empty stomach, but for some reason my wife did not make my breakfast that day so I couldn't drink.

On the 2nd March 1974, I said, 'I am going to your church', and she fixed my breakfast, but when I went downstairs, I did not want anything to eat. I was under duress; I was not myself. When I went home that night, I started to pray.

I am glad I can look in the Bible and show you where I started. Bishop Dunn was preaching and his text was Isaiah 35, where there is a highway and a way; that was his script. But as I entered the church that Sunday, I heard him say, 'See him come', and he switched as he was under the anointing of the Holy Ghost. He expounded the Word of God to let the people know that these bones, they were human beings, they were Israel, far from God. So God spoke to Ezekiel the prophet and when Bishop expounded the Word he said, 'And they were very, very dry', and tears started to run from my eyes. There was no altar call.

I went up to the altar and knelt down, then a few church members including Powell's father-in-law and another one came and Campbell was in the pool baptising people. Those two men came down to me and asked me if I wanted to be baptised. I said, 'Right now! Whether cold water or hot water, I just want to be baptised', and thence, I was submerged in the water. I was buried in Jesus' name, to rise up to walk in newness of life.

I am not going to church at present because I am not at my best in health. I know the Lord and I accept the Lord Jesus Christ as my personal Saviour. He took out my stony heart, my uncleanness, and put His Spirit within me. I have not looked back yet; after forty-one years I have not looked back. I am weak now, but I have laboured. I done my very best when I could, and as I sit down in this house I am not going to complain about anything. God has been good to me. He knew me before I knew Him. God has given a new heart and a new spirit, that you can live your life. Not for yourself, but that others too may see the Christ in you and change their way of life. What is inside will be displayed on the outside. The life that you live, people you work with and the people you associate with, they see you are a different person altogether.

So that was where I was born. The bishop was under the anointing of the Holy Ghost and he used the words 'dry', 'very dry', and 'empty'. I was an empty, empty, empty man who wanted to be filled; and praise God Almighty, I went into the pool and Elder Campbell baptised me in Jesus' name and here I am before you today. Though I am unwell, it does not bother me. If I could function right, every Sunday I would go to church, but God knows that I cannot do it. But my spirit and my mind are there, and that is the way I got into the Church of Jesus Christ Apostolic.

Herbert Harris

I AM ACCOUNTABLE FOR MY SOUL

EING SAVED IS THE BEST THING THAT has ever happened to me, though it was not easy. In 2008, I moved to London for university and one night I had a dream about the Rapture. This dream troubled me so much that I had to talk to my family, who were members of Gibson Road church where I also attend. It was then that I decided I would change the way I was living and would start going to church regularly. A couple of months down the line, I moved back to Birmingham and a few days later went on a holiday with my friends. Over the course of the holiday, I found that I could not enjoy myself and that something was missing in my life. When I returned to Birmingham I decided to go to convocation at Kelvin Way.

During the convocation, the Lord spoke to me and told me that I had been chosen and that He would make a way for me. I began attending church regularly and made the decision that I wanted to be baptised. I informed family members of my intentions; however, their reactions were not pleasant to say the least. They told me that I was rushing into it and needed to wait; and wanting to be obedient to them, I waited. Over the course of three months, which at the time felt like a lifetime, I would bring up church and baptism in conversation and their responses were continually negative; they were now growing weary of the topic. I could not help the way I felt; it was all I thought about. Being saved was the last thing on my mind before I went to sleep and the first thing on my mind as I woke up in the morning. Every time I went to church, I could feel a pulling towards the altar and with each service it grew stronger and harder to resist. I got to the point where I literally could not take it any more and decided to set a date for my baptism, despite my family's wishes. I realised that only I am accountable for my soul.

One day before Sunday service, I text my family members and prayed that they would understand and be happy for me. Needless to say, that's not what happened! I turned my mobile phone on after the service to find a message saying, *I hear that you're getting baptised; you'd better not!* I sought advice from a more senior sister who used the scriptures from the Bible to instil confidence in me. From then on, I had to sneak in and out of my own house to attend service, getting out of the house before my family woke up and coming in when they were asleep. I counted down and asked God to keep me for another week so that I could be baptised.

By the Monday, word had gotten out that I was still going to be baptised on the Sunday. I came home from my lecture (I had just started my first week of university) to find my family at home waiting for me. I was given an ultimatum to choose between God and my family; their exact words were 'If you get baptised you need to leave, but if you don't you can stay.' Without hesitation, I said that I chose God and was told to pack my things, which I did. I called my family and told them what had happened, and they insisted that I stay with them. That week, I had family members call, text, and come to university to talk me out of being baptised. One even came to church to tell an elder not to baptise me. When that didn't work, I was told that my family would never speak to me again should I go through with it. I was baptised that Sunday 4th October, and filled with the Holy Ghost on 10th November.

There comes a point in your life where, regardless of your situation, God must always come first, no matter what the consequences may be. I found the key piece that was missing in my life and was not prepared to let Him go for anyone, no matter the threat. To this day, I am tremendously blessed. I ask and it is given, I call and He answers, and I want for nothing. Truly, there is no greater thing than this!

Again, He limiteth a certain day, saying in David, Today, after so long a time; as it is said, Today if ye will hear His voice, harden not your hearts (Hebrews 4:7, King James Version). I pray that God will keep me, and that my testimony will encourage others.

God bless.

STOPPED AND LISTENED

I CAME TO ENGLAND WHEN I WAS VERY young. Being my mother's only child had its advantages and disadvantages. I attended Lozells Girls' School in Birmingham, which I enjoyed, and when I left school I wanted to be a seamstress, but that did not work out. By the time I was eighteen I went into nursing as I had developed a passion for the caring profession. As you get older, your eyes begin to open to the things around you, and you gain a sense of responsibility. In those days we had to share one bedroom; we called it 'rent a room'.

Before my mother died I met someone, got myself married and started a family, which brought more responsibility, but my life was not satisfied. There was something missing, there was an emptiness inside of me, a void. I didn't know what it was. The places

I used to go, I never used to feel fulfilled. I know I wasn't comfortable going to parties as a young woman and coming back late. I felt like I didn't belong there. Going out to make myself feel good could not fill that void. I did not feel happy and I wanted to turn my life around, so I decided to go to church. I kept searching and searching.

But one day, God spoke to me and turned my life around. He knew I was searching for something. It was one Sunday afternoon whilst coming from the swimming baths by Handsworth Park that I reached Gibson Road. There is a church there. I heard some singing, so I stopped and listened. I looked at the time and said to myself, *Church is going on at this time of day? It is so late in the afternoon!* When I looked at my watch it was just after two. I was living on St Peter's Road at the time. I believe the song that made me stop and listen was a song from the *Best of All*; *At the Cross*. So, as I was passing along and I heard them singing, the song drew me; I had to stop and listen! I always tried to settle myself at the church I used to attend, but I found that something was drawing me to this place and my life has been different ever since. It has been so different I cannot explain. I knew it was an anointed place of God, and when I reached into the church the power of God was so overwhelming! It kept drawing me and drawing me until I got involved with what was going on. I never looked at the time any more; I just wanted to get involved in the worship and God has saved me from then.

I remember when I was in the Erdington assembly it was a worship service on a Monday. But I wouldn't eat, I wouldn't drink, I wouldn't talk to anybody because they had announced that this was going to be a tarrying service and then they changed the plan. When I got home I just felt so distressed because I knew I wanted to get the Holy Ghost. It was the following week that they had the tarrying service and I went to tarry for the Holy Ghost. Whilst I was there, I prayed until there was nothing else left inside of me. Then I grew vexed and was thinking, *I need to get the Holy Ghost.* I reached out, and before I knew it I was speaking in tongues; I was speaking! I got filled with the Holy Ghost. Some people say they see this and they see that but I felt light in myself as if I was ready to take off. The sister that was tarrying with me came to me after and encouraged me and said, 'Don't let anybody rob your joy.'

Then when I came back to Gibson Road, I came to the altar to tarry and Elder Riley was tarrying with me again and he said, 'You don't need to tarry, you have already got the Holy Ghost', but I just wanted to make sure. From then on God has been blessing me. Hallelujah, God changed my life and I am now content in His blessings and favours. I'm looking back at 1972, as far back as that, and He has kept me until now. From the time I gave my heart to the Lord I have no regrets.

Sylvia Linton

IN THE MIDST OF IT ALL

I CAME FROM JAMAICA AND WAS BORN in the parish of St Thomas. My parents were Anglican. My mom usually prayed a lot and my father used to sing in the choir until he stopped going to church, but they still sent me to church. I was confirmed in the Anglican church when I was about thirteen years of age, I think it was. Even though they didn't go to church sometimes, my parents made sure, like most Jamaicans, that I went. But I used to watch my mom pray, and she usually went on her knees and told me that I must learn to pray, and also that if I done any wrong, God was going to chastise me. I used to ask what kind of whip He was going to use. As a kid growing up, that's how it was; they were very, very strict. When I went to my aunt's village, they usually went to church and it was the Church of God.

The thing is, they didn't ask me if I wanted to go to church; it was not an option, you go. No matter what other religion you belonged to, you had to go with them to church and I usually went to the Church of God churches so a lot of the hymns that we sing now, the choruses, I know them from back home.

When I became a teenager, I still had a liking for going to church on Sundays. Even when I came to England, I went to parties during the week and on Saturday nights, but Sunday morning, I just used to get up and go to church. My friends wanted to know what kind of Christian I was, because I went to church on Sundays, but on a Saturday night, I was usually at a party. I was in the Anglican church at the time so there was no restriction; you could go.

I found myself once I began to go to Gibson Road church; it's as if something was pulling me. I stopped going to the other churches and I started spending my Sundays at Gibson Road. I went there for about nine months before I was baptised. Before that, I still had my ways, still liked my blues and still loved to go to parties. But there was something about Gibson Road that seemed different from the Anglican and other churches I usually went to. It's as if something was pulling me; I couldn't explain why, but I just kept going and still went to parties, cinemas and everything with my friends. I remember Friday nights I went out with my friends and one of them had a house, so I usually stopped with him because as a young man growing up, I had no responsibilities so we just went out and enjoyed ourselves. But something seemed to be missing, because even though I went out, in the midst of it, I still got up on Sunday mornings and went to church.

Then I remember they told me that I had to be baptised in Jesus' name, and I told them that I was already confirmed. Then when I became more and more serious my friends realised that I was getting attached to this church. They kept on telling me how much money you've got to give when you go there, and what the pastor was like. They thought that he was a moneymaking man, but I told them, 'I've gone too far, man; God can save me.' You know, we were brought up to believe that people who went to churches like this (we called them clap-hand churches) had lives that were different from ours. They didn't go to parties, they didn't do what we did and so on. We always looked on them as people that were spiritual, people that were saved, different from us. But people were telling me that I had to be baptised in Jesus' name, and I said, 'No, I am already confirmed, there's no need for that.' But I remember one particular time the year I got baptised; that was 1965.

I went to convocation every day, because on Thursday my friends decided to go to London and I decided to go with them, but suddenly I found out that there was no room for me in the car, so they left me behind. So I then decided, *I'm going to go to church*, and I went throughout the week. The Wednesday, I went to the bookmaker to put my bet on and then the Thursday, I went to church as usual, but I remember this sister that said to me (and up till now I don't know who she is, and may God bless her), 'You've got to be baptised, like everyone else you know.'

I said to her, 'Where in the Bible do you find that? I'm already confirmed', and until then everyone kept on telling me, 'You need to be baptised', but they never showed me in the Bible where it says you must be baptised in Jesus' name. So she took up the Bible and showed me and said, '*He that believeth and is baptised shall be saved, but he that believeth not shall be damned*', and from the moment she told me that, I decided there and then that I was going to get baptised.

The thing is, I went and I was baptised and when I went home and told my mom, she went mad, because my family had told me before not to be baptised in that church because they'd take all my money away; they just believed it was a moneymaking thing. So when I went home they were quarrelling – man, really, really quarrelling – and the landlady said, 'His life is mash up now.'

When my friends came back from London, that is the first thing my mom mentioned to them. She went and told them, 'Lloyd is baptised.'

They said, 'We blame ourselves; we should never have left him, we should never, never have left Lloyd and gone to London; we should have taken him somehow', but you see there was no room in the car, so I had to get left behind, but they blamed themselves, and this is reality.

After I was baptised, weeks and months after, this great change came over me. I suddenly found that I couldn't go to parties any more. But I felt a lightness; it's as if I had been carrying the entire world and didn't know it, and now I was baptised it was as if I felt enlightened within. It was as if a heavy load just came off my life and then I realised this was the greatest thing I ever did. At first, I was a bit lonely because I did not know anybody in Gibson Road. I had no relatives there, no friends, nobody. I found, in the evenings, that I couldn't go out as I usually did, so I was stuck in the house and then someone encouraged me to get involved in church activities. So, when members of the church went out, I began to join them, because they went out very often in those days. On Wednesdays, I went to Derby with Elder Walrond, and sometimes we visited Dudley and places like that. When we had church during the week, I went. It took away a bit of the loneliness, because I'd had a whole lot of friends and now I was baptised, they weren't as close to me any more and I couldn't run up and down with them. I didn't have a brother, I didn't have a sister or any familiar friend inside the church.

Then one night I was going through the Bible and looked at a scripture and it said, *What agreement hath he that believeth with an infidel, or what part have idols with him that believeth, or with Christians with unbelievers?* It was as if I was praying, and I remembered the scripture, *Wherefore come out from among them, and be ye separate, saith the Lord, and touch not the unclean thing; and I will receive you, and will be a father unto you, and ye shall be my sons and daughters, saith the LORD Almighty* (2 Corinthians 6:17–18, King James Version). From that day, I separated myself from those chaps and I found myself continually reading the Bible and getting very, very attached to it. It became my companion; I was no longer lonely. I made sure I read the Bible at night before I went to bed and in the morning before I got up to go to work I read a song from the *Triumphant Service* songbook, which was the first book I bought. I got myself closely attached to the Word of God; that's why I really love it now. I keep on reading it over and over. I carried my Bible to work with me and read it at lunchtime.

One thing I found out was that with this salvation you have to have a made-up mind. You've got to really believe it to go forward. I found that I was very short-tempered. Anyone that provoked me, they would know about it and I would answer back, and in the Jamaican language some of the words we used were unprintable. But then, I remember that in my unsaved days my friends used to say to me, 'Lloyd, how come you don't swear in front of Miss Richards?' (that is my mothers' name), as it was a bad habit.

I found out as I travelled along that the bad temper I used to have calmed down, God calmed it down. The words I spoke, I spoke no more, and the short temper I used to have, I suddenly found it was gone. Now I never said completely gone, because sometimes even when I went back to Jamaica my mom said, 'You know, you're a bit touchy', but I found that I could control it, so someone could say hurtful things to me and I wouldn't retaliate; whereas in times past I usually had done.

Now that I was baptised they told me I had to be filled with the Holy Ghost. Now I did not know anything about the Holy Ghost, but I kept tarrying and tarrying and I couldn't get filled, no matter how I tarried. Many people used to say, 'We can't understand Brother Henderson, he's here Sunday, Tuesday, Thursday and he still can't get filled with the Holy Ghost', because I lived in church and I never missed it.

Then I remember, I think it was a convocation in Birmingham, it was over at Central Hall and it was in a place called Highgate. One day, Bishop Thompson (he was Elder Thompson then), the one from Canada, raised a song, *Be Still and Know that I am God*.[2] I remember he said, 'Anything that comes to my mouth this morning, I am going to say it', and as soon as he said that, something seized me and from then I was filled with the Holy Ghost.

So what I'm saying is, the road has not been easy, because you know as I said, I was short-tempered and as a young man you go to work sometimes and people provoke you regarding the colour of your skin. I was very touchy and sometimes, the way they treated blacks, something evil rose up within me to retaliate when they said something about black people, or something about my colour. But God granted me a calmness. So I found, when I was filled with the Holy Ghost, my wife Philippa was saying to me that my sons' said, 'Mom, what happened to Dad; he seems to have changed?' because sometimes when they would do something I would often snap at them. They said that I did not do it anymore and that I've calmed down because the Holy Ghost changes you, if you want to be changed.

You know something – one great experience I had (though salvation is a personal thing and you have to learn about Jesus Christ for yourself); after I got baptised, when my mom saw that I really meant it, she said to me one day, 'There's nothing wrong for you to drink, you know, because you know everyone does it; in Anglican churches they drink', but I said no. Then one day I was invited to a wedding and I went. They gave me some drink, and I drank and in the night I was sick like a dog. I was not drunk or anything like that, I was just sick and on Sunday morning I couldn't go to church and I was vomiting. My mother, who'd told me that there's nothing wrong with drinking, turned to me and said, 'Good, God ah chastise yuh [God is chastising you]; you shouldn't drink.' From that day onwards I learned: you have to work out your own salvation, don't let anybody tell you anything. Don't let anybody tell you what is wrong and right, you must be convinced within your own soul.

Then I found out that once you become a Christian, friends do not want to know you. They will often talk to you, but they push you aside. I went to church and I never found it boring, it was always a great pleasure to me. You know something; I got a little encouragement in church because people did not push me aside because I was not filled with the Holy Ghost. What they done, they told me that you have to be filled with the Holy Ghost, and they drummed it into me that you have to be filled. They tarried with me at the altar for the Holy Ghost, and they never shunned me. Throughout my life with salvation I could never, ever say one young person has said anything disrespectful to me. To be fair, if I see any young people in church, both in the past and in the present, and say that they have treated me in a disrespectful manner, God knows that I would be telling a lie. But sometimes, you have some elder people that can be very disrespectful. I found that with some of the elder ones, maybe because they had their own ways back home.

Salvation to me is one of the greatest things that has happened to humankind. The only thing is, whilst going to church, the Anglican church, I thought I was right and I was really Trinitarian to the bones, until that sister showed me in the Bible where it says I must get baptised in Jesus' name. Sometimes people can push you to the limit, and sometimes I say, *How could Jesus Christ stand by and let people spit on Him and walk away, because He's God?* You know that is one thing with salvation that I struggled with at first; vengeance belonging to God. Many times I found it a bit of a struggle, but by the grace of God, having obtained help from God, I am what I am today and I continue until this day.

I was at Gibson Road church for ten years before I got married. I'd been there for about twenty-five years before I was ordained a minister, and I'll tell you something, it was a big surprise to me that night because they did not give me a hint that they were going to do it. I know Minister Lewis used to drop a hint here and there, but I didn't take any notice of it until the night they called me, and I almost fell out of my seat. But I take it very seriously, because you find out that now your life has to be an example to others, and not just as a minister. I learned also that when I was baptised and people found out, they were watching me; my friends, you know, they watched me – 'Lloyd got saved, he's baptised' – and if I slipped up, they said,

'I thought you said you were a Christian?' You find out that once you're saved, no matter what people think, they watch you to see what your reaction is going to be. Sometimes it is not just outside; even inside the church some people can be provoking. It's not that they hate you or anything like that, but they are just provoking. But as I said, having obtained help from God I continue because there was a time when people would provoke me and they would know about it, but now God helps me.

I've been baptised in Jesus' name and filled with the Holy Ghost and continuing in this gospel is one of the greatest things that has ever happened to me. Some people say it is a bit too strict, but I never found that. I just learned that there's a difference between the unsaved and the saved. As I go along, I read the scripture, and it teaches me that there is a difference. My aim and desire is to make Heaven my home. When I look back at my life and see what I was and what Jesus Christ had done, going all the way to Calvary, my goal is to behold Him face to face and to see Him as He is.

We have a pastor who is very strict, but in the midst of it, he knows how to talk to you. If you slip up, he doesn't say, 'All right, get out the church.' He will just call you and tell you, whether it is this or that, don't do this or don't do that. But the pastor never publicly told me off. He's never called me into his office to say this sister said this or this brother said that, because God has just helped me to keep out of trouble. I didn't say that I am perfect. None of us can ever say that we have never, ever slipped since we were baptised, because if we say that, we're telling lies before God. I've faltered along the way, but God has helped me back onto my feet. Yesterday is yesterday and today is today. Yesterday's mistakes are gone, and today I go forward. I've learned from my mistakes.

One thing I have also learned is that once you are saved, the Enemy will bring things back to your mind to say, *Look, you're a Christian and look what you are doing.* He might bring back your past and the life you used to live, but what you have to do is just tell yourself, *It's all under the blood, Christ has washed all my sins away, so no matter what I've done in the past, it's covered by the blood.* No matter what the Enemy brings back and says, *Twenty years ago, thirty years ago, you used to do this,* you can say as much as you like because one thing I know for sure: what was done twenty years and thirty years ago, Christ has forgiven, and today is a new day.

In church one thing you are going to find is that you have to learn to pray. When I say pray, you know, it is not just when you go to church. Pray at home, pray at work, you can be driving and praying. You have to put time aside to meditate on the Word of God. You cannot just read the scriptures when you go to church on Sundays and put down the Bible and not read it again. It won't work, and even the songs; I don't know about anybody else, but I just cannot just go to church on Sundays and after I have finished singing in the choir, that is it – it doesn't work like that. Sometimes I just take up a songbook and pick out any song throughout the day or night, and at work I carry my songbook and at lunchtime I just read it and go through a song. Church is not just a Sunday thing; it is a thing that continues throughout the week. I learned these things because, as I said, I didn't know anybody in church so at first I was a bit lonely, but I learned to occupy myself with the Word of God and with the songs of God.

Then, one particular time, I was feeling very, very disturbed and that night I went to bed and had a dream. When I woke up in the morning, this song came to me – *All the way my saviour leads me*[3] – and since we didn't sing these songs much in the Anglican church, I had to search the *Pentecostal Hymnal* to find it. That's the first prayer song that ever came to me from when I was baptised, and I'll never forget it. I will never forget it, because I was a bit discouraged. When things go wrong, God gives you a song or a word of a scripture, He always does that. And it's not only when you are discouraged; I found out that if something is going to happen, He gives you a song for that occasion, so that when it happens, you can overcome. If you are going to go through a trial, sometimes you'll wake up with a song and you don't understand why this song keeps coming to you every day, all day, and sometimes during the week this song is just there, or this scripture is just there, until something happens and you realise that God was preparing you for what lay ahead. So that's why I said salvation is a living reality, then when you sing the song it has its meaning and the scripture has its meaning, so it's God preparing you. He doesn't wait until you get into the situation; sometimes He prepares you for the situation ahead, either by giving you a song or by giving you a word.

I have a wife that is so prayerful, she is a prayerful lady, she's always praying, always on her knees. So in our home that's how our children were brought up, they were brought up to pray all the while. Whatever they are now is up to them, but they were brought up to pray. Sometimes we prayed together and had family prayer meetings.

When I was baptised, my mom usually quarrelled with me because I went to this church. But God worked it out. God has a way, you know; the Bible says, *When a man's ways please the LORD, He maketh even his enemies to be at peace with him* (Proverbs 16:7, King James Version). She was telling me off for being baptised there but once she seen that I really meant to go on, she said, 'I hope you don't backslide. There is nothing in the world.' When I went out to church, she usually put my dinner out and got everything ready for when I came back. Whereas she used to quarrel before, now she supports me. When I took my first communion, Mom, Dad and the neighbours came out to watch me because they could not believe that somebody like me would turn around. So those who were once against me suddenly supported me and visited church, but sadly, none of them were baptised.

Nobody invited me to Gibson Road church; as I said, I went out Saturday nights, came in, and Sunday mornings, I looked for a church and I went, and then I found that once I started to go to Gibson Road church I didn't go anywhere else. I just stopped there; it's as if something was pulling me and I stayed there for about nine months before I was baptised and I never regret it, it has been the most wonderful experience of my life. Being baptised in Jesus' name, being filled with the Holy Ghost and the fellowship there was very, very great. It has been the greatest thing, being baptised in Jesus' name. A person like me who was very wild, loved his blues, loved going here and there, but God changed me and turned me around and He showed me a better way of life.

Lloyd Henderson

Four

WHAT WILL YOUR ANSWER BE?

HEN I CAME TO THIS COUNTRY IN 1962, I was living in a house with another lady and someone used to come to take her to church. Both ladies came from the same parish in Jamaica. They used to have service in a schoolroom and I used to go with them. Then one Sunday, they were singing but there was no life, yet I was still going. I remember one Saturday when I went down to the Bull Ring and a sister was talking about an incident in Jamaica, explaining how a young man was treating her mother bad, and the way she was going on! I thought, *If this is the way Christians go on I am not coming back!* and I didn't. So anyway, that Sunday evening I said to Brother Forbes (at that time he was not saved yet), 'Let me go over to another church', and when we went there, it was worse.

So I came out and I stood on the step and Brother Forbes said to me, 'Do you want me to bring you to a hot church?'

I said, 'Yes. Whose church?'

He said, 'Where Sister Harris goes' (that's Deacon Harris' wife), but it was a bit late so I didn't go.

Then on the Monday, I went down to Sister Harris's and after I spoke with her, Brother Forbes started to take me to Gibson Road church on Sunday evenings. This particular day I decided to go down on the Sunday morning. Deacon Hammy used to teach Sunday school and it was hot.

One Sunday morning I was sitting down on the sixth bench and whilst they were preaching, the voice said to me, *What shall you say, then? Shall you continue in sin that the grace of God may abound?* Just like that! But I still didn't give myself up. Then I went back early Sunday evening and I was sitting in the same seat, and the voice said to me, *What shall you do? What will you do with Jesus? What will your answer be?* I broke down in tears and I asked for baptism. At that time, they used to baptise in the tin basin. When I went back home I said to Brother Forbes, 'I was baptised, you know', and he said, 'Me give yuh two weeks' [I'll give you two weeks] because I used to love straightening my hair and whatever. I was baptised in June and I was filled in July in convocation and that was it.

I used to go to prayer meetings every Sunday morning, and one Sunday after the meeting Brother Mills said to me that Bishop wanted me to be an usher. I said, 'Me?!' and he said yes!

And from that time, I started ushering. I used to visit the sick, and wherever the young people went, I went. At that time, Elder Jones was the one who used to take the young people out and I used to go with him. I remember one Sunday when I was just baptised, I said to Brother Forbes that I was going to Manchester with the young people, and he said, 'Since when are you going out?'

I said, '*Since the fullness of the light shines in*'[4]. I didn't know that that song was in the book; no, I didn't know. Now every time I hear them sing it, I always remember. That was it.

I am going on until now. It was from 1964 until now, and I thank God. But then the Enemy tried, but I did not lie on my face, I got up and that was it.

Patricia Forbes

THERE IS A SOUND

*S*O I AM LIVING THIS LIFE, NOT BECAUSE I choose to, but because I don't really have another option. When you come to God, it is not so much because you've decided to make this change. I know people say that it's a choice you make, but that wasn't my experience. I think that when you come to God it's because He's called you to Him, and when He calls you to Him, when He actually puts His hand on you and says, *Okay, it's time for you to fall in line*, you don't have a lot of choice because nothing you do at that point outside of Him is fulfilling. There's no joy, even in the things you used to do that brought you joy, because there's always going to be that voice, that thing in the back of your mind, or in your heart or in your spirit – whatever you want to call it, it's uncomfortable. It's uncomfortable because that's not where you're supposed to be.

So, I grew up three houses down from the Church of God of Prophecy, so I've been in church my whole life really, which is weird to say because I don't come from a family of Christians. I don't come from a churchgoing family, but my grandparents would get the kids dressed and out to church on a Sunday morning. These old-school Island people – 'It's Sunday morning, put on your clothes and go church', that's what my grandmother used to say. So, a lot of Bible teachings and principles were always there and you'd be amazed at what sticks when you're a child whilst you're going to Sunday school; even the little choruses and stuff. Sometimes you randomly come up with a song and think, *Oh my gosh, I learnt that when I was seven.* But anyway, I grew up in church and I had an awful singing voice, but I loved to sing and I was in the children's choir, called 'The Gleaners'. So, that was my world, you know – church down the road and school, and that was it. But as I got older, age nine or ten, and my understanding started to improve, I was really drawn to the lessons. I was really interested in what I was being taught in Sunday school.

I was given a Bible by church and I started reading things myself, and it was around the age of nine or ten that the dreams started. I dreamed about a choice. I was dreaming about a train, and it would be the same dream every time. Sometimes it would go further, but it was terrifying because I was little and I was just learning and truly understanding about Heaven, Hell and other spiritual things. I didn't have a family to support me or aid my understanding, so I was just terrified. So I'd be standing in the front yard and the train would be going by. Basically, looking back now, that train was my choice, whether I would get on or not, and I would always let it pass. I just for whatever reason couldn't make it onto the train. But in the hills behind the house, there was a sense of evil, almost as if the Devil himself was on the hill, so I could either get on the train in front of me or be consumed by what was behind me. Jesus was on the train and I didn't choose Him. I think sometimes I wanted to get on, but I was so terrified of what was going on in the dream, it was so real to me. I was so overwhelmed by this train and this choice. Time after time, I didn't make it onto that train. You know what? Thinking about it now, so many decades later, I don't think I ever got on that train, in any of the dreams, and I can't remember what happened with the Devil on the hill. I can't remember how that part of the story developed, but I think as I matured, the dream matured because I remember watching the train from a different point (remember I said I was standing in my front yard, in front of the house), so I have memories of watching the train go by from somewhere else further down the road. I was at a different point in my life and I was literally in a different place, but the train kept coming for me, so no matter how many times I didn't get on, it kept coming back for me. He kept coming back for me. There was no *Get on the train right now or you're going to die!* and there was never any blowing of horns. I felt the urgency and I knew that I needed to get on but every time I let it pass, the dream would come back. So, I guess that came up to illustrate what I said before. When you choose to live a life with Christ, it is because you belong to Him and you can't go down any other road.

So am I the perfect Christian? Not even close. Do I live some amazing Apostolic life? No, but I know who I am. I'm a grown and sensible person. I know who I belong to and I know where I belong. I know that there are things that I can't do even if I wanted to, and that the Spirit just doesn't allow you to, you just can't get away. Once you're sealed, once that stamp is on, He owns you. He owns you anyway but there's a tangible, permanent (well, it should be permanent) link to something beyond you and you can't do certain things. You can't live a certain way, you can't say certain things, you can't treat people a certain way because I can't imagine how I would feel if I did. I can't imagine how uncomfortable and unsettled I would be. I would be disturbed for days because my spirit would be yelling, like, *Who is that? What kind of behaviour is that? That's not you, that's not how you're supposed to behave, that's not what I'm like so that can't be what you're like.* It's just like merging two people into one, and so you have one body but there are two people in there: yourself/your will and the Spirit of God.

So when I was about eleven or twelve, still living in the Caribbean, still having these dreams, still just becoming really aware of spiritual things and being really frightened by it, because 1) I didn't understand it fully and 2) there was nobody I could talk to about it, I was struggling to understand the experiences I was having. I couldn't tell anybody because I don't remember if I even knew what was really going on. For example, there was an experience I had in church one night; I think they were having like a convocation. There were services every night and there was maybe a pastor visiting from somewhere, and I think I had a night where I just got really, really tearful. Remember I told you I had an awful singing voice? I sounded scratchy and I used to have to try not to sing too loud because I was throwing the choir off key. (I tease my mother now because every time I hear her singing, I remember how I sang and I'm like, 'Please don't sing; just keep your voice down.') So anyway, it was the strangest thing. We were having something called a ten-cent march. We don't call it that here, but it is when people pay money for you to go and sing in church, to raise money. I don't know who paid and insisted that I go and sing, but the sound that came out was different from any sound that I had ever come out with before, and everybody including me was confused, like, *She can sing? Since when can she sing?*

I can sing? Since when can I sing? I can't sing. I went outside the church crying, and I remember I then had a conversation with one of my aunts. She was a Christian and she had come home to visit from the States. It was the first time I realised that I was special to God. She actually said that to me. I don't remember everything that she told me, but she saw something that evening in church. Her encouragement just made me cry more, because I'm like, *What? What's going on? What's all this? Special to God how? This is too much.*

It was too scary, it was too overwhelming, but somewhere along the line, I decided that I was going to be a Christian because it was too hard not to be. Whatever it is that makes people Christians was following me and consuming me in every way. I think one night in church I went up for prayer, and they asked me some questions, like 'Do you decide to give your life to God? Then that's it, you're saved'; at least that's what they told me. I was later baptised in the ocean (cold!), but I suspect that it was in the name of the Father, Son and Holy Ghost. I was trying to submit myself to what was happening because it was beyond my understanding. That's how my journey started. I think by then, I was about thirteen and I was well into high school.

I started high school when I was ten and then puberty kicked in and of course I rebelled. We moved house and we moved away from that church. I stopped going to church, basically doing as I pleased (without my mother finding out of course), but the voice I heard that night, the voice that showed up at the ten-cent march, stayed with me. I got involved in talent competitions, beauty pageants and modelling. I discovered boys and absolutely loved the attention. I finished high school early and was working and independent at age fifteen. I grew up really quickly after that and I moved out of my mother's house for a lot of reasons, mostly silly ones. When I was sixteen, I lived on my own. My mother was too young to be my mother and so at that age, when I needed guidance, when I needed somebody to respect and look up to, it was not her. I thought I was grown, so I went off and did my own thing. But because I was on my own and making decisions for myself, I found myself in an unfortunate situation where I became involved with somebody much older and decided that I was madly in love with him.

He was the beginning and end of the world for me. Looking back, I think it was a real valiant attempt to throw me off track because that relationship should have led to so many things that never happened. There were spiritual ties in play and I tried to get away from him but he was persistent. I was young and attached, and again because I was so independent there was nobody to stop me, nobody to intervene and say to him, 'Listen, you are so much older, and she's a teenager.' There was no big brother, there was no daddy. I grew up in a home with my grandparents, and my grandad, who was the only father I knew, had died by then. There was nobody to, I don't know, threaten him (you know what I mean), so there was no blocking him. I know now that the things that should have happened that didn't was because of that hold that God had on my life, because I'm destined for something else, because my purpose lay elsewhere. The Devil didn't have permission to do certain things, to take me to certain levels, so it was always like, *You can go this far with her and that's it*. I look back and I see how I threw myself into so many ridiculous situations where the end result seemed certain, but it wasn't, because again, you could take her this far and that's it. You know that song, I remember when I heard it the first time, I bawled my eyes out, because just those first few words... *Who taught the sun where to stand in the morning, and who told the ocean, 'You could only come this far'?*[5] That bit really, really stuck with me because look how massive and amazing the ocean is. Look how powerful and almost uncontrollable the ocean is, but then, there's someone who tells it, *This is the line*, tells the big, massive, amazing ocean that it can only come this far, and I can relate to that. I can relate to that because despite the crazy journey I've been on, God is in control.

It was a real distraction, but I kept singing. The only true joy and the peace in my life was through song and through music. I would spend, I'm sure, days on end just listening to music and singing. I soon realised that the only way to get out of what was a really messed-up situation (because I still loved him desperately) was to distance myself as much as possible from him. I could have studied law in Barbados but he would just get on a flight and follow me. However, he couldn't get on a flight, run off to England and leave his wife and child at home, as that would be a little bit harder to explain. So, even though I never admitted it to myself (and of course, I never said it to him), the decision to move to England was heavily influenced by that situation. Mostly, though, I was focused on pursuing my dream of becoming a lawyer and doing the impossible. I was the first person in my family to go to university, and getting the funding to do it is a story for another day. I was expected to be a cleaner like my mom. People actually said to me, 'You're going to amount to nothing, just like your mother', but being the 'nuff thing' that I was, I was like, *Yeah, you wait.* So it was important to me to exceed everyone's expectations. I needed to show my younger siblings as well, so they understood that we could be more than people said we were.

Anyway, I came to the UK and it was a very lonely place. I tried to fill the void on the dance floor on Broad Street. I found this club called the Rat & Parrot that played proper Island music and it made me feel like I was at home. I was struggling because I was in a world I didn't understand with people that didn't understand me. It was the closest thing that I could find to home. So every weekend (or pretty much every weekend I could afford to), I was dressed in my tight mini skirt and I would go to the Rat & Parrot and have a ball with my friends. But there was always an emptiness, so I would be in the middle of the dance floor, jammin' (dancing) to some amazing song, pretending not to feel that void, pretending that that emptiness and that hollow weren't there because if I addressed them, if I acknowledged them, I would have no choice but to cry. It would completely devastate me. The way to deal with it was to just sort of drown it out with a bottle of Smirnoff or really loud music because if I let myself think about it, I would know that the only thing that could possibly fill the void was that thing that started when I was eleven.

Anyway, a friend from university somehow ended up at Gibson Road and she was constantly saying, 'You have to come to this church, you have to come to this church.' I wasn't going to go to any church, because my experience of church in England was like a one-hour routine! You go, you read a book, you sing from the book, somebody says something, they shake a ball of smoke and then you go home, and I'm like, *I am not doing this, I don't know what kind of church this is, this English version, but fine, I'd rather stay home.* She said this church was very Caribbean.

Finally, one day, I attended service with her at the Convention Centre at Kelvin Way. It was a women's meeting and I was blown away. There was something so amazing about it. I remember I kept taking pictures. Everybody was wearing white. You know, our churches aren't like that, we don't have these colour schemes and I was just in awe, and everybody was so friendly. What sealed the deal for me was when they started singing, because there's a sound, there's a sound in Bethel that would just... I don't know. No matter how long you've been away from church, no matter what you're going through in your life, you just walk into that sound and it will do it, it will do it for you. The warmth and the homeliness I felt, it's just so... ah, what's the word? I felt like I was being rescued. You know, it's like a long exhale. Then that thing that you didn't know you wanted, just the thing that you were looking for on Broad Street, the thing that you didn't know you needed, was just there.

I don't think I went to Gibson Road consistently after that. It was a real stress because I didn't grow up in a church where you cover your head and dress a certain way because I like what I like, I want to dress how I want to dress because it's a reflection of my character. My dress and style, I decided, was a reflection of my personality and I felt like I was being challenged. Not straight away, but as I tried to commit myself to attending regularly, there were some unfortunate incidents with geriatric members of the congregation saying inappropriate and insensitive things to me. Very lacking in wisdom. I was young and new and I was clearly just trying to find my way. You have to be really careful what you say to young people because you need to let God do His thing and not try to make people fit a mould. They don't have to look like you, I don't have to have a skirt to my ankles and I don't have to wear a hat the size of an umbrella to be a child of God. I think I struggled with that because I am so independent, I'm so outspoken and I was really annoyed and didn't want to go back. There were a handful of people that made me feel so loved and so welcomed and so amazing, and that's what kept me coming back. Elder Walrond was one of those people. The man acted as if he had known me forever; I was like his friend, his daughter. I will never forget that love, and there was another mother that made me feel that way, Sister Nora Johnson. So the same friend from university was introducing me to people, trying to get me to be comfortable and become a regular member. People like Sister June Johnson and Brother Jonathan Campbell were really nice. I remember thinking, *Why are these people being so nice – is it fake?* But that's just who they were/are. God is so good because he introduced me to the right people to make that good first impression, so when the 'ugliness' came, and it does come, I was already in. It couldn't cause any damage because I was already inducted. I already knew that I was loved, I already knew that I was welcome, I already knew that I was wanted.

To conclude, because we could talk about this forever, the seed was planted a long time ago. I think it just lay dormant until God's appointed time because the work that He started when I was eleven, He needed to take a little bit further when I was in my twenties, so He brought me to Gibson Road. I look at Gibson Road as being like a school. It's like a course you have to pass before you're allowed to go into the big, bad world, for me at least.

I know that everybody's journey and what God requires of them is different, but for me Gibson Road is an anchor, it's home. So, when it came time to learn about covering my head for worship, when people said it to me it annoyed me, and in defiance I wouldn't cover my head for church because I thought, *Just because you want to look like that doesn't mean I have to look like that.* But it was a crazy experience when it wasn't them telling me any more; it was God. I couldn't deny His voice, I couldn't deny that there was something in my spirit telling me this. There was nobody around me. It became uncomfortable not to cover my head for worship or prayer. It's not some forced, awful experience. He's your Father, He lovingly directs, and sometimes it's not that it's less loving but it's less direction, and more *Do it because I said so.*

Then, you know, that led to baptism, because I question everything. I thought, *Well, I'm baptised already; what do you mean, I need to be baptised again?* The congregation and the brethren can tell you things, they can say, 'Well, this is why and that is why', but for me at least, that doesn't carry that much weight because you'll probably frustrate me into defiance. I'm not going to do it because you said to do it, and everything I've done and every step I've taken isn't because I'm trying to be compliant with anyone's 'rules', but because I've been directed by my Father to do it. So it got to the point where I knew that I needed to be baptised in Jesus' name, because as we got closer to the baptism day I just became more and more emotional. The day that I got baptised, 1st January 2006, I knew that I had to do it because it was what He was telling me to do.

It's hard, I wasn't raised in a Christian family and I still very much feel like I'm in the UK on my own. There's still so much that I have to learn about God, but I know that I belong to Him, there's no question. I know that I'm special to Him, even when I'm not special to myself. I know that He's given me many gifts, most of which are yet to be used, but He has the plan and He has the purpose. It's scary when I think about it because I'm like, *Oh my gosh, what are you going to do with me? Why have you allowed me to do this?* I think I am really anxious about His plans for me, but I know they're good for me and even if they pull me out of my comfort zone then that's what is going to have to be, because I live a life that I don't deserve, that I couldn't earn. No matter how good a person you think you are, we're nothing. We are nothing outside of God. People think that you've done so well, you're so brave, you came to the UK and you did this and that and you're a lawyer. I try not to laugh at the ridiculousness of the way it sounds, but I know that it has absolutely nothing to do with me being brave and whatever; it's my Father's direction. He has directed it and made a way, like He's done my entire life, half the time without me knowing what He was doing or what was going on.

So, like I said in the beginning, I live this life, not because I necessarily choose to, but because it is who I am. He is who I am, if that makes sense. His love and attention and care and devotion to me as though I were His only child. There is nothing special about me. There's no value on my life, aside from that which my Father puts on it. I live this life because He's called me to and I have no desire to be anywhere else, and even if I did, there would be no joy, no peace, just emptiness.

So there, we could talk about it forever; we could talk about my children and how they came to be, when I was told I couldn't have children. We could talk about the illnesses that I'm supposed to have, but don't. We could go round and round in circles talking about it, but I am where I am because God loves me. I have what I have because He's blessed me and I look forward to and am terrified of His next move, so that is the story of my life.

God bless.

PHASE 2: COGNITIVE COMBAT

I've tirelessly pursued to end this deadly cycle, and
    found I cannot do it alone.
The seeds have long been planted, it is doubt that has
    been sown.
I heard the words *Keep going*; they gave me strength but
    for a moment,
But my divisive mind prevents me from believing, and
    soon that voice grows silent.

My mind is a constant battleground; to get rest I feel I
    must shut down,
Yet even there I am still fighting; in the multitude of
    thoughts I drown.
Again, I hear an encouraging word, I know it is to help
    to bring me out,
Unfit to dwell in this place any longer, that consists of
    spiritual drought.

I know that time is receding; I know it is all in my
    mind,
For I know if I change my thoughts, God's path I will
    be sure to find.
So now I've changed my focus, God's Spirit must reign
    within,
This new mindset has broken the cycle, and this new
    journey I shall now begin.

I DON'T KNOW WHAT KEPT ME

THE FACT IS THAT I LOVED THE LORD from when I was a little girl, and as I grew up, as a teenager that love was still there. Back home in the West Indies, at school we had what you called RE, religious education. It was not like this kind of atmosphere where people are independent and say, 'I do not believe in God.' In the West Indies, whether people went to church or not, they believed in God. Now, some of us had the privilege of going to Sunday school. My parents were Adventists, so I learnt the Sunday school lesson and went to Sabbath school. I always went along with them when I was small, and then again in our schooling we had RE as our first lesson in the morning, where we were taught about Jesus' miracles and them sort of things.

But as I grew up, and once I could read, I just loved to read the Bible, especially the New Testament. I just loved the kind of things that Jesus did, you know. When reading on my own, I managed to understand as much as I could then as a child and as a teenager, and then that was it. I was just fascinated with the story of Jesus, and the part that made me cry sometimes was that He was supposed to be such a good man and yet they hated Him and done all sorts of things to Him. I used to feel so sad, and I promised myself, *When I grow up, I am going to be a Christian, so that I can be a friend to Jesus.*

You know as far as I can remember, sometimes I was going to school and got there late, because if we were passing anywhere and there was a church meeting of some sort, we had to stop! That love is just in me. Every service, anywhere in the district, where they were having concerts or Sunday school meetings, they were always inviting me. Miss Brown (my maiden name) always had to sing a song, and so I just grew up in that atmosphere and I thank God. Even though in my parish, so to speak, where I was born and brought up, you have all kinds of different churches: New Testament, Church of God of Prophecy; the Adventists were there and the Apostolic church as well, and I sort of just visited everywhere and took part in whatever was available. Although I was not a member, I could take part in recitations, sing a song or whatever, and so that was it. So for some reason, as I said, I don't know what kept me.

I was not baptised or anything like that when I was a teenager. I wasn't baptised until I was twenty-eight, but as they say, self-praise is no recommendation. I would not then dare to praise myself, but I think that the fear of God and everything like that let me live a certain way. Anywhere I went, people used to think that I was a Christian. I do not know, there was just that thing and I was so careful about how I lived. So, I did not get baptised until I came to this country, when I was twenty-eight years old and got baptised at Gibson Road. It is sort of strange with me because as I said, all through my teenage years, people were always thinking of me as a Christian and it just continued like that until I came here and got baptised. What kept me from being baptised before that I do not know, because as I said I just loved the Lord. But I did not need anybody to tell me that Jesus is God. For some reason, all those things were just natural to me. I was thinking if I'd had a choice then and someone said, 'Which of the Gods do you prefer?' Jesus would have to be number one, because even as a child I just loved the man! Sometimes I think, *Well, maybe if I was baptised when I was very young, I would have joined one of the other faiths*, which would not be the right place. I would have had the problem of being rooted in another doctrine and to change to another faith may have been more work, so in a way, it just worked out.

As a matter of fact, back in Jamaica when my beloved late husband met me he thought I was a Christian, so he did not approach me in a rude manner, it was with respect. I went to get the very first pair of glasses that I had ever worn. I went to the optician's shop and, surprise, surprise, he was not there. Now, I was miles away from home because we have what we call country and town. Birmingham is like town and then you have the country where you don't have lights and a lot of vehicles and things like that; it is more like the remote part of Britain, where people do not want to be in the city so they live in those remote parts. So I got stranded, then this gentleman riding a bicycle passed by and said, 'Good morning.' I didn't answer him because I was a stranger and all that was on my mind was *How am I going to get home? I do not want any man saying morning to me at all.* Then, strangely enough, he passed by again, and the next thing I knew he seemed to circle around another street and came back and I was still standing there. Then he said to me, 'You know, if it was a Chinese lady and I said good morning, she would have answered', so I realised he was looking for a conversation, but I don't even know what I said to him, to tell you God's truth. So that was how we met. People from the country, when you go to the city, the city people know that you are a stranger, so I am sure that was a part of it. So I managed to tell him what had happened to me and why I was there and so on and so on, and he took me to his aunt's, who did not live far away, and she went to a well-known bishop's church in Spanish Town. She was a member there, so he brought me to his aunt's house and I spent a night there.

I remember when I got back home the following day, I wrote a letter to say thank you to him because I had been stranded and was wondering, *How will I manage, how will I get back?* As I say, it was miles away and there weren't buses and trains like in England, so I wrote and said thank you to him and six months after that, we were married.

So, that's how my story of salvation goes; I just grew up in an atmosphere where we were taught about God. You go to Sunday school with your parents and that sort of thing. All through my teenage life I never focused on worldly things; I did not know what it meant to go to a party, I did not know what it meant to go to a dance, I did not know anything about that; having a boyfriend, being rebellious to your parents – I did not know anything about those things. I just grew up like that, and as I said, what kept me, I don't know. Sometimes I look back and say maybe it's because I got married young. I was twenty-two when I got married and then I had the children straight away, so maybe that was a part of occupying my mind, why I wasn't in the church much earlier. It wasn't until I came to this country in 1961 that I got baptised at Gibson Road, and the rest is history.

Nerissa Ennis

FINALLY MADE MY DECISION

I GREW UP IN A BAPTIST DENOMINATION and as I grew older, still seeking after God, I learnt more about baptism and decided to be baptised in the name of the Father, Son and Holy Ghost. Afterwards it was all exciting for the first couple of weeks, but then months after I noticed that there was still something missing. I did not encounter what the Bible teaches I would experience about baptism and newness of life. The scriptures I had studied in the Bible about baptism and newness of life I was not experiencing, so church just became part of my weekly routine every Sunday and I did not feel any real transformation in my life. As far as I was aware, I knew who God was and believed in Him. I gave my life to Him and had been baptised, yet still felt empty. So, I started to pray that God would show me something more, although I was not quite sure what I was looking for. I started to search for a different church to fill the gap, and I tried three other churches and felt no change.

A year after my baptism I met the Henderson family, who invited me to Bethel Convocation in July 2013. At the end of the service, I went to get prayed for. This was the first time I had felt the anointing from God or experienced any kind of service like that. Once convocation was over, I said to myself, *Surely Gibson Road church is not going to be as powerful as the services at convocation?* I remember as soon as I entered the church for the first time, I could feel in my spirit that this was the place I needed to be. I could feel the presence of God and my prayers had been answered. After speaking to some of the brethren and finding out more about who God really is and the importance of baptism in Jesus' name and being filled with the Holy Ghost, I finally made my decision one Sunday morning, when the preacher Bishop Mair spoke on 'Wherever you sleep is where you will wake up. If you sleep in Jesus, you will wake up in Jesus.' From that moment, I knew I could not go to sleep that night without the assurance of having Jesus, so I was baptised in Jesus' name that night on 4th May 2014.

At convocation in the same year, I was filled with the Holy Ghost and since then I can truly say I have been changed. I am not saying I am now perfect, but I know God has given me power to overcome sin by walking in the Spirit and yielding to His control. Things are not always easy, but with God directing my path, I know I can overcome any obstacle. I have learnt that there are higher heights and deeper depths to God. If you seek after Him, you shall find Him no matter who you are. If it was not for the Lord, I would still be lost with a hardened heart and no real understanding of the truth. But God is such a loving God; my experience showed me He truly cares for everyone. He answered my prayers before I even understood the real power of prayer.

Geralyn Henderson

Five

SOMETHING DREW ME

WHEN I CAME TO ENGLAND I DID NOT know many people; I knew only a few, such as Sister Benjamin and a few more people, but I could count them on my hands. But look what God has done – praise the name of Jesus. I was in a little church; they were a Pentecostal church, and they had the name, but they did not have the Pentecost in them. So I prayed to God and said, *God, I truly don't want to be one of those boys who come to England, lose their testimony and lose what you have given to them. Lord, the only thing I want you to do for me is to send me to a big church, where I just stand up, give my testimony and sit down.* That's all I asked Him. Did not God do that? Yes, He did.

I came to Number 2, Gibson Road, one Tuesday night. I felt so pressured and like I was going to give up that day. For some reason, the Lord allowed me to drive down this road, and I sat outside the church and heard worship coming from inside. It was the young people's choir. They were singing the praises of God. You see, this church, this church has a clap that nobody else can imitate, and while they were singing, they were clapping. I sat outside and I was pondering in my heart whether to go in or stay in my car and listen. But while the young people were singing I felt like something drew me from the car, and I went in and sat at the back where the deacons sat. As I sat there and listened, I thought, *This is it, this is the house of God.* Nowadays, people come to church and they just have their hands beside them, they do not clap the way they used to. I am not talking about the old ones because I can understand the older ones. I am talking about when I heard the clapping, it was the young people who were clapping and it brought the power of God down into the house. Even if the musicians did not get it right, the clapping brought it together and then the musicians fell in line. They clapped and they sang that night until I went home, and I said, *Lord, I do not want to be ungrateful, but how am I going to tell my previous pastor that I am not coming back?* because he did help me. I said, *God, how can I do that? I can't do that.* So I went to my old church and the pastor was holding a meeting, and God be my witness, I heard him say, 'Anybody who wants to leave, you can go.' I said, *Thank you, Jesus.* God heard me praying, and God put it in his mouth to declare it, so I said, *I don't have any problem; praise the name of Jesus.*

Then I went to Gibson Road and I saw the bishop. I went into his office and I said, 'Bishop, praise the Lord.' You know Bishop, how he looks at you, bright eyes focused, and I said, 'Sir, I was going to a church, but it does not feel like church to me and I do not mind coming here.'

Bishop looked at me, and he said, 'You cannot put a live chicken under a dead hen', and that was it, and from that day, I have been at Number 2, Gibson Road. God is a good God. Certainly, sometimes some people do not understand or truly appreciate what they have. It is not until you find yourself in a difficult place that you find out that what you really have is to be treasured.

Hubert Henry

HOLD ON

I CAME TO ENGLAND IN 1955 AND I came into the house where Mother and Sister Davidson invited me to church. That is how many people were saved, you know, by staying with people, living with people, talking to people; that's how it went. When I came, Deacon Taylor and my husband were living in the same place; they were lovely people and they used to talk to me. We had good talks, but I did not know about baptism in Jesus' name. I was baptised in the name of the Father, Son and Holy Ghost. But after they spoke to me, I had some lovely dreams. First, I dreamt that I was in the RAF – you know, dressed up in the suit – and we were all going out somewhere. I was dressed up and waiting outside and no one turned up. So I told it to Mother Davidson and she said, 'Go back and pray again', and the second time I dreamt that I was baptised in Jesus' name and it was the biggest pool I'd ever seen, and I dreamt that I was filled with the Holy Ghost.

They didn't have a pool, so I was baptised in a Baptist church by Deacon Bryan. He baptised me in Jesus' name and it wasn't very long before I was filled with the Holy Ghost. From that point, I never went anywhere else. I stayed in the one church because when I was back home as a young person whilst going to the Church of God, we never went anywhere, unless a group of young people were asked to go to such-and-such a church to sing. I listened to the teaching of Bishop Dunn and it satisfied me. It was a grand day when I was filled with the Holy Ghost; it was special and it was good. Everything was good about it. I never had the mind to go anywhere else but stayed right in Gibson Road; that was it and I am happy. I'm happy.

We had some really good times in church, really blessed, and Bishop done that teaching on the blackboard. It was good, it is something worth talking about. You do not lose anything when you stay with the Lord because God gives everything that is good. He said, *No good will He withhold from them who walk uprightly*, if you walk uprightly in God's sight. The world has nothing; shame is the only thing you will get, but the people cannot see themselves. Only if they give their life unto the Lord, then they can look back and say, *What I was doing out there wasn't right*, you know. They have to come to themselves, just like the prodigal boy who came to himself and said, *My father has so many hired servants and here am I* (St Luke 15, King James Version), and he returned home. I have spent some nice times with the Lord. The Enemy has been on my tail many times, but my motto is to hold on, for there is nothing better; you have nothing to lose but all to gain. From my schooldays I always loved church, always, always loved church. So, He is keeping me alive. If it weren't for God, what would I do? God alone will keep you. Keep your mind stable, and when things are getting you down, look in the holy book and have a read and sing yourself a song.

Margaret Howell

THERE MUST BE MORE

TO LIFE THAN THIS

*M*Y UNCLE DIED IN 1991, A FEW WEEKS after his wife. He went to the pub and did not make it back home; he was found in the middle of the road. I remember his daughter and I were cleaning out his house. Whilst cleaning out his fridge and putting food in the bin, I remember saying to myself, *There is more to life than this; I don't believe you live, die and that's the end of it. There must be more to life than this.* There was a particular club I used to go to every Saturday, and I remember going through a phase where I became very conscious that if a gunman came in and I was shot and died, I would go straight to Hell. So I started to hide in the corners of the club.

I was brought up in a Baptist church. I could remember my mom visiting different churches and, as I grew older myself, I found that I too visited different churches. New Testament, Baptist, Church of God of Prophecy, Jehovah's Witness Kingdom Hall, but as with the other churches I had visited, something was missing. I remember visiting a New Testament church with a friend of mine. I was waiting for the preacher to preach against sin and my lifestyle. I knew deep down that my way, the way I was living, was wrong. He preached for what seemed like two hours and never addressed my lifestyle. I was disappointed. In my teens I went to a meeting where Morris Cerullo was the main speaker; it was just all right. Another time I was pregnant, and I was with my sister outside in the old market in town, and a woman came up to us with a necklace with the Virgin Mary on it. My sister saw it as a sign and became a Catholic. I was not convinced! She was so angry with me, but I was stubborn and stood my ground. A few years later when my children were still young, a friend of mine said to me, 'What is it you're looking for? I know it's not money or a man.'

I replied, 'I don't know.'

Whilst at home, I would open the back door and look up to the sky and appreciate God's creation. The desire for alcohol left me, the desire to smoke left me. I just woke up one morning and did not want to smoke or drink any more.

I remember I had a dream; I was in a dark cave and the Devil was there. Flames were around me and came nearly to my shoulder; it was a horrible place. Not long after I went to church in the week and sat at the back. I remember the lovely feeling I felt. I did not visit the church again for a while. After that, I kept having more dreams. I put it down to something I ate the night before. I heard somewhere that if you eat cheese late at night, you have nightmares, or so the Devil had told me.

In 1993 I was invited to Gibson Road church and I went a few times with my friend who was a member at the time. I went on one of the weekdays. I felt a warm feeling from the inside and I was asked if I wanted to be baptised but I declined. One Sunday morning in 1994 I said to myself, *I am going to church today to get a blessing,* or so I thought. Whilst at the altar an elder was saying to me, 'You have no mother or father; He will be your father and mother.' More things were said, but all I kept thinking was *How does this man know my business? Should I be baptised or should I not? What if I walk out of church and drop down dead by the door; then I'll go straight to Hell.* I was not willing to take that chance, so in the year 1994 I got baptised in Jesus' name and not long after I received the Holy Ghost. This is the best decision I have ever made.

When I saw my friend again I said, 'I have found what I have been looking for – it was Jesus!' I'd tried to fill the emptiness of my soul with alcohol, cigarettes and partying, but it did not work. Jesus is the answer for all single mothers out there. Struggling, with nowhere to turn? I recommend Jesus. He will provide, deliver, heal, comfort and protect, and He will never let you down.

Jennifer Morrison

THERE IS A DAY COMING

*W*ELL, MY NAME IS SUE HIGGINS AND I've been asked to give my testimony of how I was saved, how I was redeemed, how I was delivered and set free, and how the bondage of sin was broken off me, and I suppose I should go way back; way, way back. Born to Minister Barnaby and the late Mother Barnaby, and into this wonderful Apostolic faith, blessed here around six weeks old in Gibson Road and going to church until I was sixteen, at sixteen I was given a choice by my parents: did I want to continue? I was not baptised and I stopped going to church – wrong decision, but that was the way it went. I always remember that after I stopped going to church, one of the sisters came to my family's home; it wasn't unusual for her to visit my parents. But what was unusual was that on this day, there was just me, her and I think my dad was in the kitchen, and she shut the door. And under the anointing she warned me that there was going to be a day when I would need the Lord. My back would be against the wall and I remember that she wept; I mean, she wept tears! So much so that I wasn't frightened, but I felt warned. Often over the next few years I would recall that moment and think, *I know that this is going to come, I know that there is going to be a day coming*, and it was one of them things where I just couldn't rest, and it kept coming back to me. But you know, God was good.

I left school, I had a very good civil service job, and I met my husband, Rupert Higgins, now Brother Rupert Higgins. We were married on the 4th June 1983; we met in 1981 on the 16th May. Being brought up the way I was brought up, prayer was always something that we did and actually, looking back now, I know I always believed there was a God. I always believed He existed and I didn't do anything without praying, and I can remember on our wedding day we were married in a Church of England church (long story). But I remember that the nominal prayers just didn't hit it for me, and it wasn't until we got to the wedding reception and the late Elder Dewitt Jones prayed the opening prayer that I turned to my husband and said, 'Now I feel married!' Amen – hey, what did I know? But I knew there was a greater power and I knew there was more to God than reading prayers out of a book. I knew that there was a personal relationship with Him that didn't depend on you being told what to say but it was a one-to-one connection with Him, and I suppose I craved that.

Well, happily married, I settled down into married life and some months later we were expecting our first child after about our first year of marriage. While I was pregnant, I discovered a lump in one of my breasts. I went straight to the doctor and they monitored it throughout the pregnancy and removed it after our first child Andrew was born. He was born in November 1984 and the lump was removed I think somewhere around the 9th May 1985 and turned out to be a benign cyst. They said it was nothing to worry about and I should just go away and keep doing checks. But praise God, God is so good! A year to the date I was just doing a check, and I was saying to my husband, 'It's a year since I had the lump removed, let me check', and I found another lump in the opposite breast. So within days, I was back in hospital and it was removed and again it was a benign cyst, and I knew that grace was over my life and that wasn't the day that was coming!

I knew that day was still coming, but we continued our life very happily and by then had another two children. We had Brother Callum on the 27th April 1991. Before that, we'd decided to have another child and when I went for my twelve-week ultrasound scan, the consultant told us that the baby was there but there was no heartbeat and the child had died. We were sent home to wait for the child to come away naturally, and that was a traumatic time. I believe I only got through it because my parents, who prayed for me throughout, told me that the Lord loved me, and in fact the consultant looked at Brother Rupert and me and he said, 'It's God's way of being cruel to be kind.' I will never forget it. He was a New Zealander and he said, 'Susan, it's God's way of being cruel to be kind because that child would have been so poorly it would not have had any quality of life.'

It was a testing time, a very difficult time for us because we were desperate to be parents again. We were thrilled with Andrew, but praise God, God is good and He allows us to heal, and these circumstances show us that He knew what the entirety of the life of that child would have been. He took us through that and I became pregnant with Brother Callum, and at twelve weeks I suffered heavy bleeding and wasn't sure if I would miscarry. But when they delivered Callum, they asked me, did I know that I was carrying twins, and they delivered what would have been his twin. Then we had Brother Rhys, and that wasn't without its trauma. My holiday in the US ended up with me in a six-vehicle pile-up and they said I would lose the baby. They put me on bed rest and eventually I flew home. I was pleased to be back home and praise God for all my parents' prayers.

I still hadn't given my heart to the Lord, but on my own I used to pray and I knew there was a God. Don't ask me how, but I knew. I knew there was more to life than just this everyday 'We're born, we live and we die.' When I got back from the US, they asked to see me urgently and said that my twelve-week blood test had come back and there was a high risk that Rhys would have Down syndrome. So they offered me an amniocentesis, which comes with a 10% risk of miscarriage, and I didn't know what to do. But we were assigned a counsellor – I still remember her name, Vera – and they done an amniocentesis and took the fluid to send it off to be tested. It took three weeks for this test to see if there was an extra chromosome that would indicate Down syndrome. You know, God is good because Elder Riley, bless him, whom I had known all my life, became a real comfort, prayed over me and told me, 'There is nothing wrong with that child!' He said that I should hold my faith. I hadn't committed to God, but I knew He existed.

The morning the counsellor rang me, she said, 'Your results are back, Susan, and it's a normal carrier type.' I always remember that phrase, 'normal carrier type', and I sank to my knees. As relieved as I was, I thought about all the women who would have had a positive test because I said, *God, I'm not strong enough.* God knows me and I wouldn't have been strong enough to do the other thing, which is what they would have expected me to do: to terminate. I didn't want to do that and, praise God, our child was born healthy, but even that labour, that birth was so testing in its way. All my babies were late. Callum was the earliest, at a week late.

I went into labour two weeks late with Rhys and every time I tried to deliver him, his heartbeat would disappear and they decided I needed a caesarean. They got consent forms for me to sign and I remember I said to Rupert, 'They can chop my leg off as long as this pain stops.' I signed the form but they said my signature was illegible; they had given me so many drugs I didn't know who or where I was, and they rushed out of the room to get more forms.

Whilst they were out, a lady came in, a nurse. She was wearing a nurse's uniform. Brother Rupert and I saw her, and she introduced herself and asked me my name and said, 'Are you Susan Higgins?'

I said, 'Yes.'

'You're the lady that's due to have the caesarean?'

I said, 'Yes.'

She said, 'Well, the next time there's a pain, push and let me see.'

I told her that I was having a contraction and as soon as she looked, she said, '*Stop!* The cord is around the baby's neck.' That's why the heartbeat was disappearing. Every time I pushed, it strangled him. And she said, 'Stop!' and as she said that the room flooded with what looked to me like twenty people running in and they cut the cord before I could deliver him, and Rhys was born with a less than 10% chance of survival. He was blue and not crying or moving, but they revived him.

The next day I said to Rupert, 'Please, get some chocolates and a card for the nurse who saved his life.' He brought me to the hospital and I spoke to the sister on the ward and I said, 'I need you to give these to the lady who saved the baby's life', and I described her and her uniform.

They said, 'No, nobody of that description works at the hospital!'

Now, I could understand if I was the only one who had witnessed her, but my husband was there. I believe the Lord sent an angel, and that's why I pray over all my children.

We went home from the hospital and continued with life, but I knew there was a day coming! I was getting dressed one morning and I had a wash. I was putting some moisturiser on my body and just rubbed my hand down the side of my neck when I felt a lump. 'Well,' I said to my husband, 'I've got a lump on my neck', and prior to that I had started bruising, just bruises everywhere. I had been to the doctor and they sent me off to Sandwell Hospital for a bleeding time test, where they cut you and see where the blood coagulates, but mine just kept bleeding. My platelets were broken down, but they decided it was because I had a lot of heavy colds and I had lost about five stone in weight. I had been on a diet. I was the star of the class, but the Devil knew what he was doing; he was trying to take me out and I was helping, but God is mighty, awesome and gracious.

I knew my day was coming. I went off to the doctor and she said, 'The lump won't be anything, you've had a cold. Susan, you'd never make a doctor; you're a worrier', and so I went home. I was getting weaker by the minute. I was literally crawling upstairs on my hands and knees. We had Andrew, who was nine; Callum, who was four; and Rhys, who was two. I didn't know why I was so tired, why I was so weak. My vision was going. There were so many things happening, but eventually through the civil service private scheme, they told me to see a doctor urgently.

In the meantime my own GP rang and said, 'Okay, we've decided you do need to be seen', and I went off to see the doctor at Sandwell Hospital and he did a lumpectomy where he drew fluid off the lump in my neck. He said, 'If it's nothing my secretary will phone you, and if it's something she'll phone you', and that was on the Monday.

On the Wednesday, I was at home, all my family were around; I can't remember why they were there, I think it was just the fact that I was tired and struggling with all these children. I had been to work and it was the doctor himself who called me. He said, 'Susan, your results are back, and we know it's cancer. We don't know what type, but we know it's extremely serious.' The day had arrived, and I knew that this was the day that Sister was talking about, when I would need the Lord. I looked at my three little children and I knew the day had arrived.

My mom and my dad said to me that they would care for us. I remember thinking my mom seemed so upbeat, it was almost as if she knew that I would come through this a different person, and I remember her saying to me, 'You're going to come through as pure gold.'

My husband, this gentleman, has been my dearest friend since the 16th May 1981 when we met. I have to say, you know, I thank God, I thank God for a husband who stood beside me as I went through cancer. My husband had stood when probably some men would have walked away. He has witnessed me being bald, not a scrap of hair anywhere, and weak, five stone lighter than I am now; somebody said I looked grey from head to foot. I was taken to the brink of death. I had an excess of 150 cancerous tumours. How do I know? Because I asked the oncologist if they could cut the tumours out and they said, 'Susan, we have scanned you and you have an excess of 150 tumours throughout your body.' Come on – is there not a God? We have been married for thirty-three years and God has kept us. I'd been told that I had a non-

Hodgkin's lymphoma. It was a cancer of my lymph system, and if anyone knows the lymphatic system, it travels throughout the body. The lymph is there to fight infection; if you're sick it's the lymph that in effect sends soldiers out to bring down the sickness, so cancer in my lymphatic system was bad news. There was a nurse hovering behind me as the oncologist told me what was wrong.

That was in 1995, we had been married since 1983 and in all our life together, if I ever had a problem, I would only have to look and Rupert would say, 'I know what to do, I know what to do.' When they told me what it was, I looked at my husband and for the first time in our married life, I saw panic. I saw, *I don't have the answer to this, Sue*, and I will tell you, I wasn't saved then, but I blacked out, and when they brought me round, they put me on the bed. They fanned me and they told me what it was.

We asked them, 'How long do I have to live?' and they said three months. Three months! Our children were two, four and nine, and today they are thirty-one, twenty-five and twenty-two.

My nephew, who was sixteen at the time, Elder Nick Myers as he is now, said to me, 'Auntie, this sickness has not come to kill you; it has come to cure you', and I looked at him as if to say, *Do you really understand what cancer is?* Then he said again, 'It's not come to kill you; it's come to cure you.' I looked at the wisdom of a sixteen-year-old looking through the eyes of God and giving me hope, and my mom encouraged me to go to church.

I remember the day I walked through the doors here at Gibson Road, and the atmosphere which was electric, supercharged, unlike anything I had experienced anywhere else. I grew up here, but I was looking at it with a different understanding. I sat, and obviously my parents had told the church what had happened and Bishop Dunn stood up and said that he wanted the church to fast and pray.

I was like, *Wow! These people are going to deny themselves food and everything else to dedicate themselves to prayer.* I would say the saints at Bethel and certainly at Number 2, Gibson Road, dedicated themselves to prayer for me; they became addicted to it. So much so that when I would greet them, nobody would just shake my hand and they would hold me. I remember saying to Bishop Dunn, 'So many people are telling me to get baptised, but I don't want to do it because I'm afraid, I want to do it because I believe in God, because one day I'll die. But I'm at the stage now where for me it's a reality and I want to know where I'll go.' We had this conversation at about five o'clock on a Sunday and I remember saying to Bishop, 'At the moment, if you told me to paint myself green and run down the Soho Road, I would do it if I thought it would get rid of this cancer', and he laughed.

He said, 'You know, just ask God if He's real and ask Him to reveal Himself to you.' It was specific instructions from the man of God: 'You ask Him to reveal Himself'; it was as simple as that. It wasn't a long conversation.

I went back to church on the Sunday night. I was driving home, going up the Old Walsall Road, and I prayed and asked the Lord for a revelation of who He was. I said, *I would never question you once I know, that's fine once I've got it.* I'm a creature of habit; if anybody knows me, I like to shop in the same place at the same time, every week I go up the same aisles; I like order and structure. I can't stand chaos. So I was almost at the lights on the Old Walsall Road, and when I got home, I was in the bath when, without warning, without any trumpet sound or any flashing lights, the bathroom filled with… it was… if I had to describe it, it was like a duvet being thrown over me, but with protection, love, care and nourishment. Absolutely everything for my mind, body and soul. I remember thinking, *I am not sleeping!* I was wide awake, looking at the bathroom thinking, *What?! What is this?* Then it dawned on me: *This is the presence of the Holy God.* I remembered my conversation with Bishop when he told me, 'Just ask God', and I said, 'God!' I jumped out of the water, ran into the bedroom (Brother Rupert should remember this), wrapped myself up and told Rupert, and he was like, 'What? Are you sure?' and I said, 'Rupe, I *know* He exists.'

I was baptised the following Sunday in the name of Jesus on the 20th August 1995, and that began my journey of salvation. Bishop had just preached a message, 'the three Hebrew boys in the fiery furnace', and he said, 'There are some people here warming other people's fire; what are you going to do when they take their fire home – build your own fire?' As far as I was concerned he wasn't talking to anybody else; it was just me. *The pastor's preaching to me! Oh my goodness! He's telling me I'm warming other people's fire, and there have been months of tarrying and I've done everything.* I'd worn the biggest hat to pull down on my head, and I didn't want to be rolling on the floor, I didn't want to do it. But God had to drive out some pride and some preconceived ideas. I had to get to the stage where I was so empty and so weary. This flesh that had struggled and been battered for my thirty-three years of life just surrendered.

I was filled with the Holy Spirit on the first Sunday of January 1996, and right up until receiving the gift of the Holy Ghost, the Enemy tried to tell me that God didn't want me. I remember walking to the altar and kneeling down at its right side, the side of power, and dropping to my knees. I don't know how quick that evangelist got down; she was right beside me and knelt to tarry with me. I said, 'I won't be coming back, because God doesn't want me and I am not good enough for Him.'

She said, 'That's the Devil, and you've got to rebuke him!'

And I did, and I just remember being caught up! It was almost as if my feet had left the earth's gravity, and I had a glimpse of a city. There is a city that does exist. We look at gold here, and you know, it may look good, depends on what you think, but this was a beautiful city, in colours which I have never seen in the work of any artist, no Rembrandt, no Monet. Hallelujah, glory be to God. It exists! There is a city that is prepared, streets, beautiful streets, beautiful, indescribable architecture. The Master builder, truly; Jesus is the head of the cornerstone and nothing here compares to it.

When I came back, a minister greeted me and I was saying I had been in another plane and I was wet from head to foot, and he said, 'You've been in the fire', and I remember the preaching. The journey began and it's been… if I had to do it again, the cancer was a necessary experience to teach me about my mortality and that there's more to life than this, and that there is a God to be worshipped and adored and without Him I am empty and have nothing. I needed to have that long, hard look, and I thank God for Sister Lynette Richards who was the sister that told me there was a day coming when my back would be against the wall and I would need to call on God. Because of her instruction, I knew what to do and I can say that Jesus saves and He satisfies.

When you see me worship the Lord, when you see me stand on my feet, I know why I praise God, I know why I lift Him up, because you know, God had a man, He had Bishop Dunn. When I came to this church, when I walked through those doors, Bishop Dunn asked the church to fast and pray for me; they didn't need to do it, but they did. They didn't need to afflict their souls on my behalf, but twenty-one years later I am the living proof, hallelujah, that the blood of Jesus saves, keeps and satisfies.

I would not have my life any other way and I'm blessed today to be a child of God, and after twenty-one years I could say that Brother Rupert Higgins accepted the Lord. I thank God for keeping me those twenty-one years. There were times when it was hard, coming out on my own and trying to bring three lads. I thank God that all three of them are baptised in the name of Jesus and I will say that all of my family will walk according to God's will, no matter what it is now, I know they will and I give God thanks for that, and it's an awesome blessing to know the saints. I've come to have a bigger family – Sister Marie, Sister Georgina, Elder McLean, Bishop Dunn who has been a father to me, and all the saints at Bethel. You know, those from other Apostolic assemblies and those to come. Our great mandate is to fit souls for Heaven, so that there are souls to fill Heaven. It is not His wish that any should perish but that all should come to the knowledge of Jesus Christ. Today it's a privilege and an honour to share my testimony, and to God be all the glory in Jesus' name, amen.

Susan Higgins

PHASE 3: VEILED VICTORY

I am free from my thoughts of which I was made
    captive; I now know I had to alter my mind,
For God has given me a new way of thinking, and His
    plan and my thoughts are now realigned.
Many times I was sinking in a substantial mess, covered
    in dirt, struggling for my survival,
But the mind changed, forming a new disposition, and
    caused my undisputed revival.

Frequently combating furious storms, where the waters
    seemed to endlessly batter my soul,
Why were the waters ever raging? Contrary winds
    displacing me, of which I had no control?
I finally learned to put things in perspective, and was
    made to take a different point of view,
I knew there could only be a bigger picture, but to
    understand I myself had to go through.

So now I view the mess as soil; at one point I could
only comprehend it as dirt.
It is vital for support and nutrients, you see, for plants,
dirt can do no hurt.
Those who thought that it would kill me, forgot that
plants need soil to grow,
So, thank you for providing the appropriate ground for
God to plant the seeds to sow.

You see! The floods were not to drown me, but to
provide enough water to form the river.
The dirt was not to choke me, but to force me to send
my roots down deeper.
Now I'm like a tree planted by the rivers of water to
bring forth fruit in my season,
So remember when storms are brewing in our lives,
God sends them for good reason.

CONCLUSION

HIS BOOK WAS WRITTEN SO PEOPLE CAN know they are not alone. There are many ways God can call people. We cannot put God in a box; He works when, where and how He wants to, regardless of people's opinions. God can save anybody from anything. You have not gone too low or too far for God to reach you. Why wait? What price have you put on your soul? Well, whatever is holding you back from giving your life to Christ is the value you have put on it. I don't know much, but the one thing I do know is that Jesus is real! Oppressed, Jesus will deliver you; depressed, Jesus will uplift you; lost, Jesus will find you; confused, Jesus will assist you; abused, Jesus will esteem you; rejected, Jesus will accept you; abandoned, Jesus will pursue you; broken, Jesus will heal you; empty, Jesus will fill you; suicidal, Jesus will be your reason for living.

There are times we get knocked down because of the pressures of life and the Devil will not let our souls go without a fight, but faith is unseen ammunition, prayer is a powerful weapon, and fasting is a timely missile. God can do anything but fail. There is nowhere else to go, nothing to turn back to. What must not be overlooked is that Jesus had twelve disciples. Judas betrayed Him, Peter denied Him, Thomas doubted Him, and Philip didn't know Him. If Jesus endured such things, shouldn't we? Nobody, and I mean nobody, is worth you losing your soul. As night follows day, if you seek God He will answer you. You are not too young or too old to live your life for God; God is not concerned with the age, but the heart.

This book has not been written to debate whether my God is God; to be quite honest I know who my God is – the question is, who is yours? There has to be something about this God; why else have all these people and many more had their lives changed? The testimonies speak for themselves. As an elder in our church often says, 'If your God doesn't work, try mine!' This Apostolic doctrine derives directly from the Word of God. Jesus loves you more than you will ever know. I know because He loves me, who is the least among you all. If He can deliver us, He can deliver you. You are one choice away from living the life you were destined to live.

Behold, I stand at the door, and knock: if any man hear my voice, and open the door, I will come in to him, and will sup with him, and he with me.

(Revelation 3:20,
King James Version)

For what shall it profit a man if he shall gain the whole world, and lose his own soul?

(St Mark 8:36,
King James Version)

What price have we put on our soul?

REFERENCES

1.   Dixon, J. (1999) I am Redeemed. *Heavenly News.* [CD]. USA: Spring House.

2.   Clyde, A. (1995). 'Be still and know that I am God'. *The New Century Hymnal.* Cleveland: Pilgrim Press, p. 457.

3.   Lowry, R., Burr, H. and Crosby, F. (1875). 'All the way my Saviour leads me'. *Pentecostal Hymnal.* Missouri: Pentecostal Publishing House, p. 73.

4.   Harris, T (1948). 'Since the fullness of the light shone in', *Pentecostal Hymnal.* Missouri: Pentecostal Publishing House, p. 181.

5.   Mullen, N. (2006) Redeemer: *The Best of Nicole C. Mullen.* [CD]. USA: Word Entertainment, LLC.